Such teaching as Mary Lutyens had came from governesses and a few years at Queen's College, Harley Street, London. But her real education began when, in 1923 at fourteen, her most unconventional mother took her to India and Australia and plunged her into a very different world. Her first novel was published, with great success, when she was twenty-four. She married conventionally, but without much happiness, and had a daughter. Later she added serial and short story writing to the novels she continued to produce and, in 1945, made a second marriage which has, together with her family, remained the central feature of her life.

Mary Lutyens has now achieved a second career as a biographer, having published ten works of non-fiction, all based on original sources, including a memoir of her father. In 1967 she was made a Fellow of the Royal Society of Literature. She has travelled extensively, most frequently to Venice, on which her husband, J. G. Links, wrote a well-known guide, and lives in London. The conclusion of her three-volume biography of Krishnamurti was published in 1988 and she is now concentrating his *Life* into a single volume.

'She has made of her childhood a love story which reflects life as truly as only the best novels usually do . . . a small work of art which portrays childhood as a step into life' – *The Times Literary Supplement*

'Miss Lutyens's youth was a strange blend of early 20th-century upper-class cosiness and peripatetic theosophy . . . Her mother . . . had a good deal to do with the upbringing of Krishnamurti, the young Hindu whom the theosophists had chosen as their Messiah elect, and his more active brother, Nitya, with whom Mary Lutyens was deeply in love from the age of about fourteen onwards . . . Her account of her adolescent passion for Nitya . . . is distinctly moving; and she gives you very distinct characterisations of both brothers . . . also of her own father, the architect, whose patience was often strained by the theosophical preoccupations of his spouse' – Maurice Richardson, *New Statesman*

TO BE YOUNG

Some Chapters of Autobiography

Mary Lutyens

CORGI BOOKS

TO BE YOUNG

A CORGI BOOK 0 552 99336 0

Originally published in Great Britain by Rupert Hart-Davis

PRINTING HISTORY
Rupert Hart-Davis edition published 1959
Corgi edition published 1989

This book is set in 10/11pt Linotype Baskerville
by Goodfellow & Egan Ltd., Cambridge.

Corgi Books are published by Transworld Publishers Ltd.,
61–63 Uxbridge Road, Ealing, London W5 5SA, in Australia by Transworld Publishers (Australia) Pty. Ltd., 15–23 Helles Avenue, Moorebank, NSW 2170, and in New Zealand by Transworld Publishers (N.Z.) Ltd., Cnr. Moselle and Waipareira Avenues, Henderson, Auckland.

Made and printed in Great Britain by
The Guernsey Press Co. Ltd., Guernsey, Channel Islands

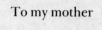

To my mother

ILLUSTRATIONS

Myself on my fifth birthday

Family group, 1908

Bognor, 1915

My mother

My father

Krishna, 1911

Nitya, 1920

Venice, 1924

Arrival at Bombay, 1924

Barbie's bridesmaids at the Savoy Chapel, 1920

Castle Eerde, 1923

Nitya in India, 1924

Leadbeater at the Manor, 1925

Myself aged eighteen

FOREWORD

This is the story of my childhood, girlhood and first love. I am well aware that my brother and sisters might write a very different account of their childhood and relationship with our parents, but each member of a family must, I think, speak for himself. This is *my* story, and it is true within the limitations of my own memory and experience.

CHAPTER ONE

Some time between the ages of three and six I knew myself to be in love. I could not have been more than six because I can see the place where this awareness came to me, a long narrow bench outside the dining-room of the London house where I was born, 29 Bloomsbury Square. My birthday is on July 31 and we always went out of London for the summer holidays before the end of July. My sixth birthday came in 1914, and when we returned to London it was to a new house in Bedford Square.

The object of my secret love (and I managed to keep it secret for many years) was an Indian boy called Nitya, ten years older than myself. I have no recollection of what he said or did on the occasion when I first became aware of loving him, but knowing myself as I was then, I can be sure that it was nothing he said or did to *me*. Being singled out for any kind of notice was not at that time a way to my heart.

Nityananda, to give him his full name, was the younger brother by three years of Krishnamurti, who was then being hailed by Theosophists as the coming Messiah. My mother had become a Theosophist in 1910, when I was eighteen months old; she had taken Krishna and Nitya under her wing when they were first brought to England in 1911 by Mrs Besant, the President of the Theosophical Society, who had adopted them, and therefore I cannot recall a time when 'the boys', as we called them, were not a natural part of my existence.

These two brothers, Brahmins from South India, were as different in character and temperament as could be. Krishna was dreamy and mystical and therefore sometimes seemed a little dense, whereas Nitya was particularly quick-witted and intelligent. They had been sent to England to be educated –

the plan was that they should eventually go to Oxford – and were under the guardianship of an English tutor, but they never stayed long enough in one place to do much work. They had no settled home, for their foster-mother, Mrs Besant, lived in India. Houses were taken for them or lent to them in various parts of England and the Continent, and when they were in London they stayed with a very rich American, Miss Mary Dodge, whom Mother had converted to Theosophy. Later Miss Dodge settled on them both an income for life.

We spent the summer holidays of 1913 together at Varengeville, in Normandy, and I just remember the picnic we had there for my fifth birthday. I was crowned with white roses and was very conscious of my happiness and importance. We did not stay in the same house as 'the boys', but we saw them every day. In looking back at Nitya, I can see him only as he was in the years I knew him best, but I do not think he changed very much in appearance, though he certainly became extremely well dressed, which he was not when he first came to England.

He was short and slightly built, with a skin the colour of milk chocolate; straight black hair; thick, rather frowning, eyebrows; beautiful hands and even more beautiful feet. (In childhood the feet of one's playmates are as familiar as their hands.) But it was his mouth I remember best. It gave the impression that at any moment he might burst out laughing. And indeed he did laugh a great deal, though not perhaps as much as Krishna, who, in spite of often seeming vague to the point of stupidity, could be vitalised into the most infectious laughter by jokes and funny books.

Although I had known from my infancy that Krishna was destined to become the World Teacher, I felt no great reverence for him in my early years. On the contrary, when he entered our nursery we would greet him with the jingle, 'Cowardy, cowardy custard, your face is the colour of mustard; your hair is black and greasy too; cowardy, cowardy custard' – a rudeness which he always took in good part, though, unlike a real brother, without retaliation. He was particularly fond of me, the baby of the family, and made a great pet of me, so it was a sign of my perverseness that I

12

should fall in love with his brother, who, as far as I can recall, took no notice of me at all when I was a child. Nitya was fond of my eldest sister, Barbara, who was his own age, and for the first few years after coming to England he and Barbie were close friends. She and my brother Robert, who came next to her in age, were both interested in Theosophy at this time and saw much more of the 'boys' than we little ones did.

Theosophy was the philosophy on which I was nurtured – that is, the belief in reincarnation and *karma*, that inexorable law by which you reap what you have sown of good and evil through a succession of lives (I was brought up to think of good or bad *karma* rather than of good or bad luck); the equality of all the great religions, and, since 1902, a conviction that the World Teacher was shortly to come back into incarnation. It was the great Lord Maitreya – he who had taken the body of Jesus two thousand years ago and founded Christianity – who was, in the near future, to take the body of Krishna, my friend and almost-brother, and sow the seed of yet another religion.

As a Theosophist, Mother became a strict vegetarian, and we children (there were five of us) were brought up as vegetarians in accordance with her principles. Even our nanny became a vegetarian because she could not bear to refuse us the little bits of her breakfast bacon for which we begged. As no animal fat was allowed in our cooking, our food was fried or roasted in a white vegetable grease called Nutter. Unlike some vegetarians we were allowed eggs, but nuts and cheese formed the major part of our diet. We bought nut-cutlets from Shearns. They were in the shape of real cutlets and had a piece of raw macaroni sticking out of them to look like a bone. A mixture of grated pine-kernels and thin honey was my favourite breakfast dish.

The only member of the family who did not become a vegetarian was Father, so there were always two sets of dishes served in the dining-room. Theosophy caused a rift between Father and Mother which did not heal until I grew up, and I think it was this widening gap between them which made Father seem so remote from me throughout my growing years, for I stood on Mother's side of the breach. I was always afraid of being left alone with Father and of having to make

13

conversation to him. He had had the effect, ever since I could remember, of making me feel particularly dull-witted. The others had seen more of him in their childhood than I, partly because until 1910 he had had his office on the ground floor of the Bloomsbury Square house, and partly because it was not until 1912 that he began to go to Delhi for the winter months every year to build his new city. As he only once came with us for our summer holiday, and as I had all my meals in the nursery, there was little opportunity of seeing him, and yet my first distinct memory is of him: on the day of King George V's coronation he came up to the nursery and cut crowns out of orange-peel for our dolls.

We saw him on Sunday afternoons, it is true, when we went down to the drawing room after lunch. It was his turn for amusing us, and he got out of it rather unfairly, I used to think, by offering a shilling to the one who went to sleep first. Naturally he went to sleep first himself, but it would be only a short nap, and when he woke he would draw wonderful pictures for us – some of them on folded paper which opened up to reveal surprises. Pictures he drew at the dining-room table, made realistic with the help of mustard, had the disadvantage that they could not be kept and treasured. One of these, a particular favourite, was called The Relief of Lady Smith and can no doubt be imagined.

But I enjoyed watching a drawing being born even more than the finished picture. He would make a line here, a line there, or a couple of circles: what was it going to be? From the smile on his face it was apparent that he himself could see it plainly on the blank paper and was already enjoying it and our ultimate delight in it. I have always resented my inability to draw, knowing how easy it was for him. He used to tell us about a small boy who when asked how he could draw so well replied, 'I just think and then draw a line round my think.' It was obvious that this was the way Father drew.

Sometimes on a Sunday morning he would take us to the Zoo, of which he was a Fellow, and we would go behind the lions' cages, and see the seals specially fed for our benefit, but in truth I was very bored by the Zoo. I did not much care for animals. For years Mother kept a Pekinese which she pampered, and this dog would allow you to stroke it and then bite your hand when you took it away. When I was eleven I was given a fox terrier of my own (called Joseph because I was Mary) but he did not show me the exclusive devotion I felt entitled to from a dog, and when I found that he left worms on my bed I gave him away. Earlier I had been given a black-and-white Japanese rat, called Methuselah, but Mother soon took possession of him. He lived in a three-storeyed house in her bedroom and utilised each floor for a different purpose. When Mother was called in the morning his front door would be opened and he would come jumping up, first on to the stool at the foot of her bed, then on to the high bed itself, and then he would run to her and snuggle into her neck. He lived for more than two years and finally died of consumption from sitting in his bread and milk.

Although Mother was often away from home lecturing for the Order of the Star in the East, an organisation which had been formed in 1911 to proclaim the Coming of the Lord and of which she was National Representative for England, I never felt that she neglected us or was not there when we wanted her. To me she was the perfect mother. I would not have liked her to dose me, bath me, comfort me or hold my head when I was sick. These intimate functions were performed by Nanny, who had come to our family when Barbie was born in 1898, or by Annie, our nursery-maid, who had come when I was three and was therefore, I considered, my own special property. I did not like Mother even to see me in the bath, and as for other relatives, apart from sisters, I would not for anything have allowed them to see me undressed. As well as being very modest I had a great sense of my own dignity. It was torture to be left in the lavatory with the door unlocked and to have to shout when I was ready. I think I should have died of shame if a stranger had come in.

Mother never seemed to miss an evening in coming up to say goodnight to me in bed, when I would go through an undeviating ritual of telling her how beautiful she looked. She used to come up dressed for dinner in a long Fortuny tea-gown of soft accordion-pleated satin, her five-pointed gold star, the emblem of her office as National Representative, gleaming on her breast. She had two of these Fortuny tea-gowns, one in black and one in sea-green, which she wore alternately. The sea-green was my favourite, and even today I cannot imagine a more beautiful dress.

Every morning I would go down to a little room which we called her shrine-room, where she used to sit draped in a yellow Indian shawl, burning incense in front of a Crucifix and a statue of the Buddha, and I would hold her hands while I recited a prayer which began, 'I am a link in a golden chain of love which stretches round the world and I promise to keep my link bright and strong.' (I said it like a parrot, without any thought of the tremendous promise I was making.) She would then read me a chapter from a little book written by Krishna called *At the Feet of the Master*, and afterwards a passage from the New Testament. Theosophy did not exclude Christianity or any other religion; it taught you to live your own faith. Indeed Mother instituted ordinary family prayers, which the servants attended, after the move to Bedford Square, and she used to allow Nanny to take us to church, and our governess to give us normal Christian instruction. My own conception of God was certainly conventional enough. He had a long white beard and his Christian name was Harold. He could see everything you did, even in the lavatory with the door locked, and he also knew what you were thinking, so it was no good trying to hoodwink him.

After tea Mother would come up to the nursery to read to us. I have never known anyone read aloud as beautifully as she did. Not only was her voice gentle and full of expression, but she possessed to perfection the art of skipping. She read to us only the books she loved and knew so well that she knew just where to skip a dull passage before she came to it, so I never knew when she was doing it and did not feel I was missing anything. She always knitted while she read, and occasionally she would drop a stitch and have to pause to pick it up. We accused her of doing this on purpose at the most exciting moments to increase our suspense.

Before I was nine and a half (I can date this accurately because we were evacuated to Shropshire in February 1918, and when we returned to London it was to yet another house) she had read to us all Jane Austen (most of them twice and not a word skipped); a great deal of Dickens; *Vanity Fair* and *Henry Esmond*; *Wuthering Heights*; *Jane Eyre* (I can still hear

16

Mother's beautiful voice ringing out passionately: 'Jane, Jane, why do you torture me?'); *Uncle Silas*, and a great deal of Bulwer Lytton, Anstey, George Birmingham, Kipling, Saki, Rider Haggard and W. W. Jacobs.

Of the children's books she read to us I particularly loved *Little Mother*, *The Secret Garden*, *Treasure Island*, *Holiday House*, *Castle Blair*, *The Magic Valley*, *At the Back of the North Wind*, and two little books written by our aunt, Mrs George Wemyss, called *All About All of Us* and *Things We Thought Of*.

Alice in Wonderland was not a favourite. I was outraged to discover at the end that it was all a dream, and I have never quite forgiven it. Other people's dreams are always boring. And it was so unnecessary too, because there was nothing in Alice's adventures which could not be readily believed. They were intensely real. I demanded a sense of reality in books, just as I always strove for verisimilitude in my own imaginings. Successful fairy-stories must have this power to suspend disbelief. For instance, there is no difficulty in accepting the fact that Father Christmas comes down the chimney, whereas to believe that he comes through the key-hole would put a great strain on one's credulity. He could, of course, make himself small enough by drinking a potion or reciting an incantation, but *how would he get his sack through?* It *might* be explained, but a satisfactory explanation would have to be given. Imagination has its own laws.

Before Mother started to read of an evening she would ask us questions about what had gone before and reward us with coffee-beans for the right answers. It was one of the great compensations for being the youngest – indeed the only compensation I can think of – that I did not have books read to me which were thought suitable for my age. I never found what Mother read above my head, and I was certainly never bored for an instant. I took what I could or what I wanted out of it and let the rest go without any straining after greater understanding. I daresay I missed some of the finer shades of style and meaning, but I do not think I enjoyed a book any the less for that. Thus Jane Austen was purely romantic to me; I was quite unaware of her wit and irony, and yet of all the books Mother read to us, including children's books, *Pride and Prejudice* was by far my favourite, perhaps because of the unique fascination of Mr Darcy.

Mother used also to sing to us – songs she had sung to the guitar in her youth, such as *Golden Slippers*, and *We Sat upon the Baby on the Shore* and *Polly Wolly Doodle* – but she had given up playing the guitar by the time I came along. My favourite among her songs was one which began, 'Mary's been bewitching me, oh, that naughty Mary.' When she sang it to one of my sisters she would substitute her name for Mary, but I was gratified to think that it was really addressed to me. She also had a rhyme which I loved:

Oh, do you know the Starling?
He's such a perfect darling;
For when you're feeling weak and ill
He comes and soothes you with his bill,
And when you're feeling ill and weak
He comes and soothes you with his beak.

Nanny used to read fairy-stories to me out of the Coloured Fairy Books, but she did not read nearly as well as Mother, and I could tell that she was bored, which Mother never was because she never read us anything which bored her. But Nanny, to make up, had a wonderful repertoire of Victorian songs – *The Old Arm-Chair, My Grandfather's Clock, Little Tottie Went to Ma, The Lights of the Harbour, Johnny Sands* – and many others which I liked even better than Mother's songs; and to sit on Nanny's lap and be sung to while she rocked me to and fro like a baby was a treat which I went on demanding long after I had grown so big that I almost squashed her. To be sung to without sitting on her lap was not the same pleasure.

Nanny and Annie had both been brought up in the Guards' Home, an institution where a wonderful training in all the domestic arts was given to the daughters of Guardsmen. Annie was very musical and could play the piano beautifully. Her father was a drum major. Nanny's father was keeper of the Robin Hood Gate of Richmond Park, where we used to go and have tea with him occasionally in his lodge. She also had three sisters called Lil, Lal and Lol (she was Lou), and a fireman-brother who showed us over

18

his fire station on one thrilling occasion. He was killed in the war, and his death was my first contact with sorrow.

Nanny had been with only one other family before she came to us – the Gippses – where she had started as nursery-maid. I do not know how many children there were in that family but I heard of only one – Lulie – and Nanny only left the Gippses because Lulie got married. I hated this unknown Lulie Gipps whom Nanny loved so much, and was always hoping that Nanny would say something unkind about her; but she never did. Because she could not bear to leave Lulie, Nanny had turned down a proposal of marriage from a young man called George. Would she do the same for us?

CHAPTER TWO

Elisabeth, the sister next to me in age, whom we always called Betty, did not get on with Nanny, though it seemed to me that Nanny was always an angel to her, but Betty declared that Nanny was so highly strung that it made her even more excitable than she was by nature. Nanny certainly had wonderful vitality, but I found her personality very soothing. Betty and I are examples of how little environment and upbringing influence the intrinsic character of a child. We could not have been more different, although we were brought up in an identical way. Betty felt very strongly that Mother neglected her. Not sharing my affection for Krishna, who invariably brought Nitya in his wake, she was jealous of Mother's intense devotion to him. (Mother made no secret of her obsessional love for Krishna.) And then she hated being read to, principally because she could not sit still. She suffered from growing-pains in her legs, an affliction I accepted as a recognised complaint, just as I accepted the fact that I had hollow legs which enabled me to eat more than any of the others. (I had a marvellous digestion – perhaps because Nanny used to let us run round and round the table directly after meals playing an ever-enchanting game called *Pass* which consisted simply of crying out 'Pass' whenever we passed each other.) But above all Betty was bitterly resentful of being lumped together with me as 'the little ones'. I used to think, even when we were small, that she had every justification for her resentment, for like most children I had a strong sense of justice.

In a family of five there is bound to be an odd one out, and by rights it should have been me. There were two years and three weeks between Betty and me, whereas between Betty and our next sister, Ursula, there were only a year and nine months; and yet Betty was made to go to bed with me, share a night-nursery with me, dress like me and do everything with me, whereas Ursula, far from being left out in the cold, which would have been some compensation, seemed to be given all sorts of almost adult privileges. To make it even harder for Betty, I was very tall for my age as well as fat, so that strangers sometimes mistook me for the elder.

No wonder Betty had screaming-fits. She had been born at breakfast time, hence her love for porridge, and her screams at three weeks old had frightened away burglars. When she screamed now it was still usually in the middle of the night. Her tantrums enlivened my childhood and I thoroughly enjoyed them, though I like to think that if she had been punished for her misbehaviour I should not have relished it so much; but as far as I remember she never was. In the night when she woke screaming, there was always Nanny's prompt reassurance: 'It's all right, darling. Nanny's here. Hold Nanny's hand.'

Once, just after we had gone to bed, Betty screamed for Father, who promptly came when he heard he was wanted, although he did not usually come up to say good-night to us. As soon as he appeared at Betty's bedside she yelled at him, 'Go away, you horrid man,' and he went as fast as he could. I enjoyed this incident more than any of the others, even though, or perhaps because, I was very awed by it.

I admired Betty's naughtiness immensely, and more often than not I adored her, but I knew that when she lost her temper and we fought, she fought to kill. It was lucky for me that I was the stronger, for her rages were terrifying. One day in the country she tried to lay me out with a golf club, and if I had not dodged the blow and then got hold of the handle and wrested it from her she would certainly have stunned if not killed me. And on another dramatic occasion she threw a knife at Mother across the dining-room table and missed her by a hair's breadth, but this was some years later, after we had been promoted to dining-room lunch.

Only once do I remember her being obedient. Nanny had told her to sit still, so she sat immovable for a whole morning with her back to the toy-cupboard. We beseeched and raved at her in vain. Said Betty, 'I was told to sit still and I'm going to sit still. I'm a very good girl.'

21

But her remorse was as swift as her temper. We were for ever making it up with protestations of undying love. She would give me all her favourite toys during a reconciliation, but take them back again next day. However, she accused me of never giving her anything at all except a cold in the head.

On Sunday nights she and I used to take it in turns to enjoy the doubtful treat of sleeping in Nanny's bed till ten (it was most unpleasant then to be moved back, half-asleep, to one's own cold bed), and invariably when my turn came I would share Nanny's pillow with a little note in Betty's enormous scrawl begging for Nanny's forgiveness. She was far the most generous of us and had much the most vitality, but she also had a capacity which seemed very strange to me, and not wholly admirable, of being able to play with toys of completely different sizes and species in the same game. Thus she could accommodate a large doll and a tiny lead animal in the same piece of make-believe, something which I was quite unable to do. In my games everything had to be to scale.

When she was nine she went to a boarding school at Westgate (she was the only one of us, including my brother, who ever went to a boarding school) where she stayed for five years with certain privileges not granted to the other pupils. She remained a vegetarian; she was allowed to have her own dog, a white Pekinese, and to have me to stay with her occasionally for a week-end; her letters were uncensored and it was understood that she could leave the moment she wanted to.

Betty's naughtiness had the effect of fixing in me a consciousness of my own extreme goodness. I was the easiest child imaginable for someone like Nanny to handle, but that was because my predelictions usually happened to coincide with the mild rule of the nursery. Nanny was wonderfully reasonable in her dealings with us. For example, we were not made to put away our toys while a game was in progress. We would play on the nursery floor, sometimes together, but more often in separate corners, and could keep our toys there for hours or days or sometimes even weeks – at any rate until that particular game palled and we started to play with something else. Nanny never interrupted us if she could possibly help it when she saw we were absorbed, but when she

22

did tell us to do something or not to do it, I, at any rate, usually obeyed her.

An incident had occurred some time before I was six which gave me a great respect for Nanny's authority. I had been given a swing for my birthday and when we returned to London after the summer holidays it was hung up in the night-nursery in Bloomsbury Square, but it was not hung in the right place; it was too near the dressing table, which could not be moved because of the light. Nanny said she would get the carpenter to change its position as soon as possible but in the meantime I was not to swing on it or I would surely put my feet through the looking-glass. This seemed to me silly. Of course I would not break the glass. I wanted very badly to go on my swing and decided to do so in defiance of Nanny's orders, though naturally I would be careful not to touch the glass. But hardly had I begun to swing when both my feet crashed into the mirror, shattering it to splinters. I was not hurt but I was quite dreadfully shocked. I forget whether I was punished or not, but certainly the shock was quite punishment enough, and even worse was my sense of dismay that my judgement had been at fault. Nanny had been right. Nanny knew best. Grown-up councils had prevailed.

There were only two repeated conflicts between Nanny and me. One was over the question of going to church. Every Sunday afternoon I would say to her, 'Need I go to church next Sunday?' and always she would answer infuriatingly, 'We will wait and see,' which was no good to me. I must know my fate, so all through the week I would repeat the question about twice a day, and each time receive the same maddening answer. If it happened to be wet on Sunday morning, or if Nanny was feeling particularly indulgent, I was allowed to stay at home, and this happened more often than not, but occasionally it would be, 'Yes, come along, darling, to please Nanny,' and in spite of the winningness of her tone I knew there was an inflexible will behind those words and that I would have to go, though in the worst of tempers. I think the truth was that Nanny liked to go herself and could not bear to be parted from me, but as a special treat she never made me go to church on Christmas Day when we were at home.

It was to St Pancras Church that we went from Bloomsbury

23

Square, and not only were we allowed to come out before the sermon but Nanny provided us with tiny picture books to look at all through the service, so it is unreasonable that I should have disliked church so much, but it was the one place where my imagination could not function, perhaps because of the distraction of continually having to stand up or get down on my knees.

The other clash between Nanny and me came only once a year and was to do with the putting on of winter combinations. Every October I would writhe on the floor in fierce and furious protest against this abominable form of clothing, but Nanny always won the battle, and into combinations I went. (It would never have occurred to me to appeal to Mother for a dispensation, although I might have gone to Nanny to appeal against some order of Mother's. Nanny was my ultimate authority.)

My reason for disliking combinations so much was a valid one, I think, for not only did I hate the feeling of the thick wool next to my skin, and the sense of restriction which the one-piece garment gave me, but I felt them to be unclean, as indeed they were. The joy of coming out of them, however, which I was allowed to do at Easter, whatever the weather, almost compensated for the misery of going into them.

It was this natural sense of cleanliness as much as anything else that made me so amenable. I was uncomfortable with dirty hands, actually enjoyed cleaning my teeth, and was so fond of my clothes that I hated getting them torn or dirty. I looked upon them more as toys than as clothes and took violent likes and dislikes to them, especially to my shoes which all had human faces; and I preferred to pick my nose rather than dirty a lovely clean handkerchief.

Another characteristic which made me so easy to manage was that I was never bored so long as I was left to my own devices. I had a great power of concentration and could amuse myself for long stretches at a time with just one toy. There was one doll in particular called Ruthie who had a very large trousseau (she really belonged to Barbie, but I thought of her as mine and did not have to ask permission to play with her), and I used to sit peacefully on the floor by the hour, day after day, dressing and undressing her. She was the chief joy of my Bloomsbury Square years, and her charm would no doubt have carried on to Bedford Square if it had not been for an unfortunate occurrence. I had an accident in my drawers one afternoon after tea – the worst kind of accident. Such a thing had never happened to me before, as far as I could remember, and the horror of it outraged all my most sensitive feelings. The wise thing to do would have been to go straight to Nanny or Annie and confess what had happened (it was the last thing I would have been punished for), but it was too terrible and shaming to put into words. Instead it seemed to me that if I could succeed in forgetting it, it would cease to be (I believe this reasoning accounts for many a child's failure to own up), and therefore I went for forgetfulness to my chief source of pleasure – Ruthie – and sat down quietly on the floor and began to play with her. I did not succeed in forgetting my dreadful predicament for an instant; it was discovered when I went to bed (I can remember Nanny saying in a tone of surprised concern, 'But why didn't you tell Nanny, darling?'), and the permanent result was that I turned against Ruthie. She had become the embodiment of all my horror and shame.

But in nothing was my apparent docility more in evidence than in going promptly to bed when bedtime came. The truth was that I liked going to bed, for in bed as nowhere else I could indulge in my most beguiling form of play – telling myself stories of which I was the hero. There was never a heroine. My first hero was a boy called Spirits who wore a white satin suit and played the fiddle and went to parties where he turned water into lemonade. Even now when I cannot find a book of an evening to suit my mood I fall back on going to bed and lying in the dark telling myself the story I would like to read.

In winter we went to bed in firelight – real firelight from an open coal fire which made red-and-black patterns on the walls and ceiling – a joy unknown to the child of today. How cosy it was, how safe, how enchanted. The night-nursery door was left ajar, and across the landing Nanny and Annie would be sitting in the day-nursery, also with the door open in case we called, having their supper or doing our mending or ironing. (I can so clearly see Nanny in her high, boned net collar and wide, white starched belt with the silver filigree buckle, her black hair puffed out with pads that lay on the dressing table at night; and I can see Annie's sweet, pretty, kittenish little face, but not what she wore.) They never stopped working for us, which seemed only natural and right in my beautifully ordered little world. But at least I repaid them with abounding love. It is related in a letter from Mother to Father how, at the age of four, when I was given a fluffy toy with a label stuck on it saying, 'With luck,' and I asked Nanny what luck meant and she replied, 'Having lots of nice things,' I threw my arms round her and said, 'Lots of you, then.' I was never in any doubt as to how much she meant to me.

I do not remember her ever speaking crossly to me. When I was naughty she would say sadly, 'You hurt Nanny,' which had far more effect. Being sent to bed early was the only punishment ever inflicted on us, Mother and Nanny both taking the view that if we were naughty we must be ill, and if we were ill bed was the best place for us, but even this was enforced with a very gentle firmness. And it was no punishment at all to me, though naturally I did not let on to the fact. I never hesitated to dissemble when it suited me, and did not have the slightest sense of guilt in doing so. I was perfectly tractable so long as I was led in the direction in which I secretly wanted to go.

So parents, beware of good children. Beneath their docility may lurk a crafty and ruthless pursuit of their own ends.

CHAPTER THREE

We were at Sulhampstead Rectory in Berkshire, which we had rented for the summer holidays of 1914, when the war broke out. The war was brought home to me far more forcibly when the pony who drew the lawn-mower was commandeered for the front than by the news that one of our Lutyens cousins had been killed. We seldom saw our Lutyens cousins, although there were a great many of them, and I never knew my Lutyens grandparents. Father had been one of a family of twelve – eight brothers and three sisters, with an adopted niece, the daughter of his widowed eldest brother, thrown in. Father himself was the youngest boy but one. His godfather, Sir Edwin Landseer, had wanted to adopt him as a child and I always had a secret regret that his mother had refused to let him go.

We rarely saw any of his family except his sister, Mrs George Wemyss, our Aunt Mollie, who had written those two enchanting books for children, recounting the naughty doings of their large family. Occasionally Father would appear in the nursery in a top hat and morning coat, and Nanny would tell us that he was going to the funeral of one of his brothers. He had had a brother called Daisy – it must have been a ninth brother – who had died at the age of eleven after converting a Jew to Christianity. This was Father's own story which greatly intrigued me, but I have never discovered how much truth there was in it.

Father had suffered greatly in his boyhood from having clothes passed down to him from his elder brothers, and this gave me a fellow-feeling for him, for my own clothes were passed down, not from Betty, fortunately, who wore her clothes abominably, but usually from Ursula. She wore her clothes very well, but when she was wearing anything I

27

particularly coveted, I would watch her with the greatest anxiety to make sure she took proper care of it.

Father used to tell us a story about wearing his brother Fred's cut-down trousers on his first day at a new gym class. The trousers had merely had the bottoms of the legs cut off, so that the fork came somewhere near his knees. When the boys were ordered to put their hands on their hips, the instructor came up to Father and roared, 'You're deformed. Go straight home.' But Father talked very little about his boyhood, and most of what we knew about it came from Aunt Mollie's books.

When we returned to London in the autumn of 1914, it was to our new house, 31 Bedford Square, which nobody but I seemed to like. Our night-nursery looked out on to the Square, but the large day-nursery was at the back, facing west, with a fine view of chimney-pots and the Y.M.C.A. tower in Tottenham Court Road. The move made little difference to my routine, for we still had a Square garden in which to play. The Square meant a great deal to us because we were allowed out there without hats or gloves, and in summer we took our tea there and went barefoot. (How strong were summer sensations. There was the warm smell inside my straw hat, and the thirst at bedtime, unquenched by tepid water from the bedroom jug.)

The house was supposed to be haunted, and now among its ghosts must be the spirit of my own intense happiness during the three and a half years we lived there. I *knew* I was happy and revelled in it. Paper angels had taken the place of Ruthie. Father used to draw these angels for me in coloured crayons and I would cut them out but not stick them on cardboard because their very limpness was part of their attraction. I had dozens of them, all about nine inches high, all with golden wings and golden hair, but dressed in different coloured robes. No drawings of his can ever have given more delight than those angels gave me. I have forgotten what story I wove around them as I sat on the floor playing with them day after day, but I palpably remember the marvellous joy with which they filled me.

The happiness of my childhood did not, I think, fit me for adult life, but it is a lovely thing to look back upon. Happiness

28

in childhood is more nearly perfect than any later happiness because it is unalloyed by the faintest sense of guilt or self-criticism or apprehension that it may not last; moreover it is blessed with the radiance of unimpaired health and the fineness of unblunted senses.

My happiness came primarily, I suppose, from my imagination, but also partly from my sense of complete security. (It was characteristic of me that I always thought the gate at the top of the nursery stairs in Bloomsbury Square was there to stop intruders coming up.) Or did it come from my good digestion or from the fact that Mother had nursed me for almost twelve months? I was waited on hand and foot; I never had to do a chore; my meals came with punctual profusion; I was surrounded by love, sympathy and, unlike Betty, by justice. As for being understood, it suited me far better not to be. And everything that was done for me I took for granted as my natural right. It was never pointed out to me that I owed gratitude to anybody or that my security depended entirely on Father's brain and capacity to work. At the age of four I was heard exclaiming to myself, 'The world is my kingdom,' which so exactly represented my outlook that it is hard to believe I did not know what I was saying.

But although I was given a greater sense of security than any child could possibly have today, my life would have been considered very dull by present standards. We seldom went out to tea or had children to tea with us; I never went to the cinema until well after the war; I was never taken to a pantomime, and it was not until 1920 that I saw *The Beggar's Opera*. (I then saw it twice.) We went once a year to *Peter Pan* with a friend of Father's, and I was taken once to *Chu Chin Chow* and once to *Where the Rainbow Ends* by the same lady, but these were not my greatest treats because they involved a social obligation, either a lunch beforehand or a tea afterwards, when one had to be on one's best behaviour and render thanks to one's hostess.

My greatest treat was to be left alone in the nursery on a wet winter's afternoon with the curtains – large pink roses on a grey background – drawn against the murk outside, while Nanny and Annie went off together to Bourne & Hollingsworth. Then I would become one of my angels and leap about

29

the room in the firelight pretending to fly. When I heard Nanny's footstep on the landing I would go and sit quietly on the stool by the high fire-guard. Nanny would open the door and say, 'Why are you sitting in the dark, darling?' The light would click on and magic would vanish.

Occasionally we went to a party – usually at Christmas time – but this meant taking my hair out of plaits and undressing to the skin in the middle of the afternoon in a cold night-nursery (for the fire, even though lit, had not yet had time to warm up the room) and putting on clean underclothes, including a starched petticoat with lace round the top that scratched my neck (Nanny always made us put on clean underclothes too before a journey in case there was an accident); and when I got to the party, conversation with the new children I met there was confined to the three questions: 'What's your name? How old are you? What time do you go to bed?' I was terrified of crackers and would, if I got the chance, secretly pull mine to pieces and hide the banging part under my plate, but I loved to watch the red gelatine off the outside curl up in the hot palm of my hand as if it was alive.

I did not need other children, although I got on quite well with them. When picking up sides for a game I was strong enough and could run fast enough not to be left to the last, which would have hurt my vanity, but through all the games I played with other children, the story I was currently telling myself would go on in secret in my head. Hide and Seek and Red Indians were very suitable for this, but there was practically no game that did not serve my secret purposes. Card games, however, were more accommodating than any others, because my hero, in whatever guise he found himself, was always a reckless gambler.

Sweets were as lacking in our lives as entertainments. They were said to be bad for our teeth, so apart from one chocolate after lunch on Sundays we never had any, and I certainly never felt the lack of them. My pocket money for years was sixpence a week, but I do not remember ever buying anything for myself, though naturally I was obliged to buy presents for the family at birthdays and Christmas, and occasionally induced to put a farthing in a box for Waifs and Strays which Nanny kept on her chest of drawers and which had on it a

30

picture of two ragged orphans clasped in each other's arms for warmth.

I once took something off the counter of our favourite toy department in the basement at Gorringe's, but made the mistake of proudly showing it to Nanny when we got home. She insisted, in spite of my protests, on my taking it back next day, only relenting to the extent of allowing me to tell the saleswoman that I had taken it by mistake instead of confessing that I had stolen it.

I was a natural miser and after some years of hoarding was able to change my money into a beautiful five-shilling piece, which I kept in a miniature leather trunk and gloated over at least once a day. When I was twelve, carried away by a sudden rush of love for Ursula, who had had an operation for appendicitis, I spent all my money, including my beloved five-shilling piece, on a small leather vanity case for her, which I very much regretted almost immediately afterwards. (When Father came to me on my wedding morning with tears in his eyes and a cheque for two hundred pounds and said, 'Pay it in quickly in case I change my mind,' I knew just how he felt.)

Nanny used to extract a pound from Father for our birthdays, which went straight into the Post Office. 'Extract' is the right word because she would stand over him until the note was reluctantly produced, but perhaps, knowing that Nanny would never fail to remember our birthdays, he could safely forget them. One Christmas, when we were staying with our Lytton cousins, Father doled out five-pound notes to them on Christmas morning, and then, turning to me, said, 'I suppose I shall have to give you one too.' I took it in the spirit in which it was offered, but I am sure he would have been better pleased if I had refused it.

Father, though, had much more justification than I to be careful with his money. He had come from a poor home, and the fear of poverty must have hung over him for many years before he achieved success, whereas nothing I wanted as a child was ever withheld from me. I am sure Nanny would have given me out of her own money the toy on the counter at Gorringe's if I had asked for it.

But perhaps I reached the apogee of happiness in Bedford

31

Square when I had jaundice. After the first few days I stopped being sick, and although I remained bright yellow for some weeks (a condition which Nanny enhanced by tying the ends of my plaits with yellow ribbons), and was confined to bed, I felt as well as could be. My bed was moved into the day-nursery, another instance of Nanny's wisdom, so that I should not miss anything that was going on. In the early mornings Annie would come in to do the nursery grate before breakfast, and as I lay on my side watching her we had some very interesting conversations. I loved having her to myself like this and hearing all about the Guards' Home. It was a glorious moment when the fire was first lit and, because Annie had laid it so expertly, at once blazed up. Then a basin would be brought to me so that I could sponge my face and hands and clean my teeth, and I would be all ready, clean and neat like the grate, for my Allen & Hanbury's Diet for Invalids, which I adored and always called by its full name. Afterwards my paper angels were brought to me on a tray and I would play with them until lunchtime. I had complete peace of mind; I was escaping lessons and in no danger of having to go to church. What could be more blissful? I never wanted to get up and was delighted when I had a relapse just as my convalescence was drawing to an end.

CHAPTER FOUR

I have said nothing about the joys of Christmas because the enchantment of that day is much the same for all children, and ours differed from the normal only in that we hung pillow-cases at the end of our beds instead of stockings. When we staggered with their delightful, bulging awkwardness down to Mother's and Father's bed at eight o'clock on *the* morning (fancy them not wanting to be called until eight even on Christmas morning!) I came into my own for once as the youngest by being allowed to open my presents first – exciting brown-paper parcels glimpsed on the hall table before Nanny whisked them away to be kept for *the* day. One of Betty's parcels once turned out to contain some old underclothes forwarded from her school, the only argument I can think of in favour of the modern use of decorated wrappings. Nanny would open each of her presents with the comment, 'Do to give away next Christmas,' and straightway it would go into her bottom drawer. Father used to greet everyone who came to the house on Christmas Day with the question, 'Have you heard the news? . . . It's a boy!'

We sometimes spent Christmas with our Lytton cousins at Knebworth House in Hertfordshire. This would mean hiring a station horse-bus from King's Cross (I can still smell its exciting mustiness); our huge brown nursery trunk with its rounded lid would be put on the top and as we started off we would sing in pleasant melancholy, 'Goodbye, London, Good-bye, London, the prettiest little London that ever I've seen.'

Lord Lytton, our Uncle Victor, was Mother's brother. Of our four cousins, Hermione was Ursula's contemporary and special friend, and Davina was mine; while poor Betty suffered another injustice by being paired with John, who, much as we loved him, was the baby of the family. Antony, the eldest, was a young god who always took the name-part in our games of 'Ogre'. Knebworth was very stimulating to my imagination. It was a huge old house with battlements, towers, a minstrels' gallery, a haunted room, a spiral staircase and knights in armour at the foot of the slippery dark oak main staircase. The whole house had a heavenly smell – wood-smoke and furniture-polish mixed with its own individual essence – which I came to regard as the authentic smell of Christmas Eve. Knebworth is the prototype on which the great houses of my imagination have always been founded.

But I did not like the day-nursery there as much as our own. The entire carpet was covered with a white drugget fastened down with huge brass-headed studs, and this somehow gave the room an insubstantial, temporary feeling; and the Lytton Nanny governed with a more formal rule. Moreover it was no fun playing with other children's toys (I have always had a great sense of possession and would far rather give something away than lend it), and I did not like their rocking-horse nearly as much as ours because it slid backwards and forwards on an even keel instead of rocking properly on curved bases as ours did. Our own rocking horse, down whose pummel-hole most of our cherished small treasures had vanished, could be rocked so violently that it would advance at quite a speed over the carpet. Then the Lyttons had on their nursery wall a large picture of Peter and Wendy flying over the roof-tops, which I considered very babyish and inferior to *The Boyhood of Raleigh* in our own nursery. Besides, the habits of our cousins were different from ours. For instance, they were given milk and Coronation biscuits before bed, whereas we were never allowed a mouthful after tea. They had stockings instead of pillow-cases on Christmas morning, and did not open their big presents until after lunch, and as Nanny held back our presents when we were staying there, not only did we have to wait for them until after lunch but we did not have the contents of a stocking as a stop-gap. Worse than anything, I could never get out of going to church. The Lyttons had a family pew with high walls which gave me claustrophobia, and Nanny did not dare give us picture-books to look at. The only diversion was that Uncle Vic read the lessons.

Most winters there was skating on the lake for all the neighbours and villagers as well as for the Knebworth house-party. Uncle Vic was a beautiful skater and it was he who decided when the ice was thick enough to hold us. When he gave the word a crowd of volunteers swarmed on to the ice to sweep the snow away, and everyone who was equipped to do so would follow Uncle Vic's example and don Swiss caps, scarves, gloves and boot-trappings. There was a small fishing cottage by the side of the lake with a thatched roof and brightly painted furniture which the Lyttons had brought back from Norway, and here we would bake potatoes in the ashes of a wood-fire between sessions of skating.

There was also a racquet-court at Knebworth which was fitted up as a gymnasium as well, with a gallery for onlookers, and one of the favourite amusements of the children staying in the house was to sit on the gallery rail, holding on to the rope which was suspended from the ceiling of the court, and jump out into the open, swinging on the rope. I longed to do this too but never found the courage. I became aware very early in life that I was a physical coward, but this did not worry me much. I accepted the disability as I accepted my fat legs and straight hair. I was not particularly ashamed of it and felt no compulsion to try and overcome it, though had I been a boy it would no doubt have caused me much unhappiness and shame. I never wished to be a boy, any more than I wished to grow up. For years I was called Baby, which I liked, and protested against the use of my Christian name. I protested too at being ousted from my pram: long after I should have been using my legs Annie wheeled me about in a push-cart. I saw no reason why she should not continue to do so indefinitely. I never liked walking, and when for a time I had to wear surgical boots to correct a tendency to turn my feet out, it was really painful. I had imitated a girl I saw walking with her feet turned out almost at right angles, which I con-sidered most distinguished, but the imitation soon became second nature and took many months to rectify.

In spite of the luxuries and excitements of Knebworth, I was always delighted to get back to my own nursery. I grew up thinking that our own habits, practices and prejudices were the only civilised ones, and that we had the most brilliant father, the nicest nanny and the most beautiful home and mother of any children in the world.

CHAPTER FIVE

It was probably Mother's reading so much aloud to us, and my habit of telling myself stories, that made me particularly backward in learning to read. I could not read *with ease* much before I was ten. The first book I ever read to myself with pleasure, though not with ease, was Beatrix Potter's *The Tale of Mr Tod*. It took me more than three-quarters of an hour, in the night nursery in Bedford Square, from a quarter-past seven when I got into bed until eight o'clock when we were what we called 'shut up', and then I had to beg for an extra five minutes to finish it. I was very proud of my achievement. I had at last mastered, more or less, an art which had caused me great anxiety, boredom and frustration. I have never had a more difficult bridge to cross. I remember asking Mother very seriously one day when I was about eight whether I must really go on with this appallingly difficult and hated lesson, and she, with equal gravity, promising me on her word of honour that if I persevered I would find it worth while. Spelling I never mastered and like to think is of no importance. There is a blessed complacency in most of us which soothes us into believing that what we cannot do is not important. The unlucky minority feel that it is only those things they cannot do which *are* important.

Probably another reason I found it so hard was the intense dislike I had for our governess. Barbie and Robert went to a co-educational day-school – King Alfred's in Hampstead – while Ursula and I had a P.N.E.U. daily governess whom we called Bernie. Lessons were done in the dining-room in Bedford Square and some other children came to share Bernie with us. We had one terrible lesson called Brushwork when we had to paint seascapes in watery blue and sepia. (Why must I stick to sepia when there were such lovely colours in my paint box, particularly the strawberry-and-cream mixture of white and crimson lake?); and another called Picture Study, which consisted of sticking black-and-white postcard reproductions of all the great pictures of the world into an album. (When first I went to Florence, years later, memories of Bernie in her green overall and pince-nez came between me and most of the pictures there.)

We also had a French governess who came two afternoons a week and whom I also disliked intensely. She had very large yellow teeth like old piano-keys which were much in evidence when she tried to teach me to say *Un œuf, des œufs*. At *œufs* her teeth were revealed in a skull-like grin. I do not think she appreciated Father's irregular French verb as much as we did:

> *Je pense*
> *Two pense*
> *Three-pence*
> *Pensions*
> *Rendezvous*
> *Restaurant.*

As well as these lessons we attended weekly sessions at McPherson's gymnasium in Sloane Street and dancing classes at Madame Vacani's, both of which I very much enjoyed; and then, once a fortnight, a tall, grim widow – I have never seen a longer, blacker figure – came to the house to teach me scales. I cannot say she taught me the piano, because during all the months we put up with each other not once did she play any kind of tune or allow me to play one. Her tuition, however, lasted longer than it might have done, since Annie used to do my practising for me. She was glad of the opportunity to exercise her fingers while I sat on the floor beside her playing with my toys. The alacrity with which I went to practise was held up as another example of my extreme goodness. The widow, I think, must have noticed that I made absolutely no progress, but doubtless she did not wish to lose a pupil. She looked half-starved as it was.

That was the extent of my musical education, for when the widow left, no one came to take her place. I was never taken to a concert or to an opera (except for *The Beggar's Opera* years later), nor did I hear any good music on the gramophone, with the single exception of the *Unfinished Symphony* which had somehow found its way into the miscellaneous pile of nursery records between *The Wreck of the Troopship* and *The Broken Doll*. Until Betty went to school she shared the grim widow with me with equally poor results. At school she took up the violin as a therapy for biting her nails, and that was the start of her musical career.

My dislike for our governesses was, I am sure, unjustified, though fully reciprocated. Ursula flourished under them. But then she must have been a very rewarding pupil and all her teachers adored her. Although we shared governesses and a day-nursery, there were not only four years between us but almost as much difference in temperament and appearance as between Betty and me. Ursula was blessed with curly hair and was always very popular with grown-ups; she was Father's acknowledged favourite (Nanny tried to soften this for Betty and me by explaining that she had been so delicate when she was born that it was feared she would not live), and she was also a favourite with his artist friends; and yet I had no envy of her. I did not envy anyone. I realised even then that few people, whether children or adults, shared my heaven of never being bored in my own company.

As for the other members of the family, Barbie, the eldest of us, ten years older than myself, was as remote as Father. I knew nothing of her life and stood in great awe of her. I was proud of her beauty, and the fact that Nitya loved her gave her an added glamour in my eyes. She sometimes interested herself in our appearance and made spasmodic efforts to see that we were better dressed. All our clothes were made either by Nanny or by a sewing woman, Miss Drake (Father called her Miss Sew-and-Sew), who came to the house three days a week and whom we all loved very dearly. One day Barbie said that she thought I might look better with a fringe, and proceeded straight away to cut one on me, but as I have a very high, prominent forehead the fringe stuck straight out at right angles. Barbie's comment was, 'She looks even worse,' and thus I was left until the fringe grew out.

Our only brother, Robert, three years younger than Barbie, was the object of my deepest love and admiration, and I never tired of hearing Nanny recount the naughty things he had done when he was little. Once when he had been sent to bed as a punishment he had plastered the walls with porridge. On another occasion, just as he and Barbie were about to set out for a party, he had released a clockwork motor-car in her hair which it had taken Father three hours to untangle. (How extraordinary that it was Father who had the patience to do this!)

Robert was wonderfully gifted. He played the violin; he could play anything on the piano by ear; he had a beautiful singing voice and he could paint; but when he came into the nursery it was usually to tease. He immediately tried to see which of us, Ursula, Betty or me, he could first reduce to tears. I was very proud of myself because I was always the last to succumb, and very often did not succumb at all, whereas his mere presence in the doorway was usually enough to set Betty off. There was a cane-covered bench in the nursery, and standing on this we used to have wrestling matches with Robert, and here again, owing to the size and firmness of my legs, I held out the longest. All this had an effect on my character. I came to look upon self-control as the greatest of the virtues and gained a reputation for hardness of heart which I relished. Before I was ten I had adopted as my motto, 'Know all but be known of none,' from Basil the Agnostic. How quickly one grows into a reputation! My secretiveness was natural but my hardness a deliberate cultivation.

CHAPTER SIX

In the summer of 1916 we spent the only holiday with Father that I can remember. One of his own houses, Folly Farm in Berkshire, was lent to him by the client for whom he had built it, Mrs Merton, a rich lady of German extraction. It was a holiday of unusual gaiety and activity, with people constantly coming and going and as many as ten or twelve of us at times to play Crazy Croquet. (Father was a serious croquet player but he never minded joining in Crazy Croquet on occasion.) I loved croquet. The balls had strong personalities. Yellow was my favourite; I tolerated blue and red, but if I had to play with black I could not even try to win.

Folly Farm made on me a deep impression of luxury, beauty and fitness. The very eiderdown of rich satin on my bed was luxurious beyond anything I had ever known. For the first time my aesthetic sensibilities were stirred and I realised that rooms could offer something more than comfort and convenience. Knebworth was beautiful inside, but I had known it ever since I could remember and its size and romantic trappings were what appealed to me as a child. It was not until much later that I came to appreciate the perfect taste with which my aunt had embellished it. Folly Farm had also the appeal of newness. It still smelt of new wood, plaster, fresh paint and turpentine from the brand-new murals in the dining-room.

Nanny went away for a fortnight while we were there. She had almost to be pushed out of the house before she would take a holiday – in fact it is the only time I remember her going away – and I am sure she missed us even more than we missed her, for we had the compensation of receiving either a post-card or a parcel from her every single morning she was away – a doll's jersey which she knitted in the finest tie-silk on the finest steel needles or a souvenir from St Leonards.

Barbie, who was now eighteen, was a nurse in an army hospital at Waverley Abbey, but she spent some of the time with us at Folly Farm and had a string of friends to stay. William Nicholson was also there for much of the time. It was he who was painting the murals in the dining-room. I could not bear Nicholson, in spite of the fact that he carved perfect little violins for Betty and me out of wood. He was like a mischievous monkey with the mischief directed towards oneself, and he said clever, sharp things. But I fell in love with his wife, Prydie. As with Nitya I am sure it was nothing she said to *me* which made me love her; for I needed no return beyond the opportunity of being in the presence of my beloved. She used to play the pianola in the long gallery for hours at a time, and I would sit unobserved on a window-sill watching her in perfect contentment, sometimes for as long as she stayed there herself. I wonder if she had any idea what this small girl of eight was feeling for her. I am sure I gave her no sign of it. I never saw her again after that summer, and, alas, two years later she died.

I also fell in love at Folly Farm with one of Barbie's friends, a tall, fair girl who wore a kilt. I do not use the words 'in love' loosely. I *loved* many people, but very different was this unpredictable magic of in-loveness, under the influence of which the mere presence of the beloved produced a joy so intense that when he or she so much as went out of the room for a few moments one was left with the desolation of home-sickness.

But these passing summer fancies did not change my constant, underlying in-loveness with Nitya, and if he had been there I do not think I would have been fickle; but neither he nor Krishna came to Folly Farm. I saw very little of them during the Bedford Square years, because for the most part they were at a crammer's in Kent. The idea of their going to Oxford had been abandoned and the plan now was that they should go to London University. Nitya went to France as a dispatch rider for some months.

I do not believe I ever thought of Nitya when he was not there in those early years. His presence was joy to me and I felt desolate for a while after I parted from him, but I did not miss him, nor did I try to find out when I might see him again. I should have been too frightened of giving my secret away for one thing. But I kept my ears open for any mention of his name. In his presence my shyness was as intense as my happiness. I did not dare look at him. The ideal situation for love such as mine had been in the long gallery at Folly Farm while my beloved played the pianola. Her back was to the window-sill on which I sat, so I could gaze at her to my heart's content. I do not think she ever knew I was there.

Some time during 1917 Nitya came to live on his own in a flat in London, in Dover Street I believe, and was looked after by a former parlour-maid of ours, an old dragon called Walters. One day when he came to Bedford Square he asked Nanny and me to go to tea with him in his new flat on the following Thursday. I know it was a Thursday because it was my gym day. I was in a glow of excitement from the moment we were invited, and on the day itself I felt there was nothing I could not accomplish. I paid unusual attention to my morning lessons, and at gym that afternoon how high I jumped, with what verve and vigour I marched and climbed the rope and swung my Indian clubs.

We went straight from the gym to Nitya's flat, but when we got there we found he was out. He had forgotten we were coming. Walters gave us tea nevertheless, and I remember a kind of sweetness, in spite of my grievous disappointment, at sitting in his room, surrounded by his things, lapped in the charm which he and Krishna created round themselves wherever they went. For one thing they were so much cleaner than anyone else I had ever come across (cleanliness had always had a special attraction for me), and their slim figures so much better dressed (they went to the best boot-makers, tailors and shirt-makers); their neat brown shoes were always so beautifully polished, and their straight black hair, which was parted in the middle and smelt of some delicious unguent they both used, so sleek.

I suppose these two brothers seemed more alike than two English brothers because their foreignness set them equally apart. Their English accent had an identical lilt and their laugh the same rather high-pitched tinkle. (How irresistible I find an Indian accent in English even today.) They had such beautifully flexible hands too. They were both able to bend the first joints of their fingers without bending the second. (I have since discovered that many Indians can do this.) Nitya was not as classically good-looking as Krishna, but his face had great charm and his smile was irresistible. He had a very slight squint under his thick eyebrows, which was an added attraction rather than a blemish, but curiously enough I did not discover until years later that he had been born with the sight of only one eye. What else can I say about him, except that he had a tiny hole in one of his front teeth through which he was able to squirt water? As I had a space between my two front teeth which was useful for the same purpose we once had a match to see which of us could squirt the longer jet.

I remember hurrying Nanny away when Walters told us that if we waited she was sure Mr Nitya would be in soon. I did not want him to come back and find us there unexpected, unwanted; which shows a child's natural wisdom. Nanny was inclined to be cross and to think he had been rude to us (she was very jealous of Mother's devotion to 'the boys'), but this I would not allow. I made out that I was glad he had forgotten, as it had enabled us to have our tea in peace. All we had wanted was to see his flat. It would have been a bore to have to talk to him if he had been there. My secret must be preserved at all costs.

Another unhappy episode – one of the very few I remember while we lived in Bedford Square – had also to do with an invitation to tea. We had there a pretty, Irish Roman Catholic housemaid, called Eileen, with whom I was in love during Nitya's absence at the crammer's. She used to let me ride on her back when she was down on her knees brushing the blue hair-cord carpet in Mother's bedroom. One day to my great delight Nanny asked her to tea with us in the nursery. That afternoon Nanny and I set out, as we usually did when it was fine, for the Green Park on the top of a No. 14 bus. (The top was uncovered in those days and there was a mackintosh rug to pull over one's knees if it rained.) The bus was involved in some kind of accident just by the Ritz and all the passengers were made to get off. This did not worry us, for the Ritz was our stopping-place anyway, but Nanny suggested after our walk in the park that as a treat to make up for the accident (as if the accident itself had not been treat enough) we should go and have tea in a favourite shop in the Burlington Arcade where we sometimes had macaroons on a Saturday morning. (Nanny seized on any and every opportunity to give us little extra treats.) For fear of revealing my love for Eileen I was unable to remind Nanny that she was coming to tea, although common politeness alone should have made me do so. I knew how sensitive Eileen was and how hurt she would be at our forgetfulness, but I could not say anything. We had tea in the Burlington Arcade, my disappointment almost choking me, and when we got home it was as I had feared; Annie told us how Eileen had come to the nursery at five o'clock in her best black silk and how hurt she had been because we had forgotten her.

Soon after this Mother asked in a priest to exorcise the evil which everyone but I seemed to feel in the house. He went from room to room intoning prayers and shaking what Annie called his holy-water-rattle, while Mother followed behind, swinging a censer. The whole house reeked after-wards of incense, which brought on one of Nanny's bad sick headaches. All the other servants made such fun of the priest that Eileen was deeply outraged, and she was indig-nant too that Mother had not asked him to go into the servants' quarters. She declared that he had simply driven the evil spirits from our part of the house into theirs. She left the next morning in high dudgeon. I stood on the landing and watched her carry her Japanese basket down-stairs. She wore black kid gloves and her eyelids with their fair lashes were still pink from her indignant weeping. She would not say goodbye even to me, and though I was crying out in my heart, begging her not to go, I could find no word to say to her.

What is this instinct which impels so many children to keep their deepest feelings secret even to the point of great pain to themselves? Is it that they fear ridicule, or that they intuitively know that what lies at the bottom of their hearts is so delicately sacred that at the first breath of common air it will fall to dust? Or do they hide their hearts as a dog buries a bone? The expression 'childlike simplicity' has always seemed to me absurd. Children are not simple. They are motivated by instinct and therefore it is impossible to know what is going on inside them by paying heed to their words or observing their actions, for as often as not these are uttered and performed to put you off the scent. With the

45

growth of reason instinct dies away unperceived, and that is why so few adults remember what it was to be a child. Their minds cannot tell them nor their adult hearts. As well remember the human race before there was speech.

CHAPTER SEVEN

In February 1918, when I was nine and a half, the most important event of my childhood took place. Ursula and I, with Nanny and Annie, were sent off to Church Stretton in Shropshire to get us away from the air-raids, and there I remained for the next eighteen months. The war had impinged very little on me, and if it had not been for the wounded soldiers in their blue cotton uniforms who came to the Square to play bowls, and a Belgian family of refugees who occupied part of the ground floor of our house, I should hardly have known it was on until the air-raids started, although I was sufficiently conscious of it to tell Mother that I thought it unpatriotic to do lessons in wartime.

The air-raids were tremendous treats, when we were taken down to the kitchen in our dressing-gowns and there fed on scrambled eggs while we played Racing Demon. (I never went into the kitchen at any other time, and never at all into the servants' quarters upstairs.) Nanny would take her treasures down with her in a peacock-coloured satin Dorothy bag, which she called her Zeppelin bag, and though we nagged her endlessly to tell us what was in it she never would. I always suspected that it contained a photograph of George.

Before the move to Church Stretton there had been two changes in my schooling. Ursula left Bernie to go to King Alfred's, where Barbie and Robert had been, and although I continued to have lessons with Bernie the classes were moved from our house to the John Buchans' house in Portland Place. Alice Buchan was my own age, but her two brothers were younger, and I remember nothing of this period of my education beyond buttoning up their gaiters every day for the walk we took at break. And then for a fortnight I too went to King Alfred's. There was the excitement of the long tube

47

journey to Hampstead, and the beauty of my new school clothes – a pleated skirt, and jersey to match, in a lovely lovat green. On my first morning a boy was sent out of the room for whistling in class. Hardly had the door closed behind him when someone else started to whistle the same tune. I was thrilled by such blatant naughtiness, and then frozen with dismay as I found everyone looking at me and realised that the shrill noise was coming from my own lips. The teacher looked embarrassed as she said, 'We must excuse Mary as it is her first day,' but I am sure she believed she had a little devil to deal with.

Our headmaster, John Russell, had lost all his hair in an earthquake, even down to his eyebrows and every eyelash. One morning he appeared in a wig. He called the whole school together and addressed them in some such words as these: 'Yes, as you see, I am wearing a wig. A wig is a very ridiculous thing and you will want to laugh at it, so I suggest that you laugh now. Laugh as much as you want to.' There was not so much as a titter then or at any other time. Although I seem to remember this incident vividly, I do not think it can have happened during the fortnight I was there. I was probably told about it, and it so impressed itself upon me that it became part of my own experience.

I suppose our evacuation to Shropshire was the main reason why I stayed such a short time at King Alfred's. When we first arrived at Church Stretton we went into lodgings in the Carding Mill Valley, a couple of miles out of the town, but later we had our own little house, Holly Cottage, just outside the valley gate. It was a very narrow valley, between whimberry-covered hills, completely wild in those days, and running through it was a full frolicking stream which rose on our moors and eventually joined the Severn. When it rained the wild ponies would come down from the hills and stand disconsolately by the stream. Apart from a couple of lodging houses just inside the gate (which was there to keep the sheep in) there was only one house about a mile up the valley, where the old mill stood; this too had lodgings to let, and was kept by two old ladies, Miss Gamble and Miss Roberts. Here there was a big pool where we bathed in summer and skated in winter. Past the mill-pool the road narrowed and soon divided into

48

two steep paths, Mott's Road and the Lightspout, both leading up on to the moors. The moors were so wild that I seldom ventured up there by myself, and in the winter snows people sometimes got lost up there and died of exposure.

I have been back to Carding Mill Valley recently and wish I had kept away. The stream has dried up and charabancs go up as far as the old mill, which has been turned into a tea-room with a machine outside showing What the Butler Saw. But in spirit it is still my valley, where no child ever pretended with more intensity of delight. From the afternoon we arrived and immediately rushed panting up the hill opposite our lodging-house windows we had almost complete freedom. No more hats, no more gloves, no more church, and best of all we were allowed to wear breeches with *pockets*, a luxury which cannot be appreciated by anyone who has not for years kept his handkerchief and his treasures up the elastic of his bloomers with the constant danger of the elastic giving way and all the treasures being scattered on the ground. I must certainly have appeared an absurd figure in old black riding breeches of Barbie's, the black matching jacket, worn over a jersey, sticking out round my hips in a kind of frill; my long plaits bobbing on my chest and my fat legs encased in roll-top stockings above K-boots (the day after we arrived we went into the town to buy these boys' stockings and boots); but what did I care what I looked like?

From the first we instituted high tea to give us a longer afternoon, and from a diary which I kept for three days in March, I find that we had 'hiy tea at six with fried Fedjerter-beles and Fermersilly and Roles and Setrar Setrar.'

A great friend of Ursula's, Elizabeth Downes, who was staying at Miss Gamble's (it was Elizabeth's mother, Lady Downes, who had discovered Carding Mill Valley and lured us there) introduced us to her Scotch riding-master, Mr Pringle. He was short, broad and bandy-legged, with twinkling blue eyes in a red-brown face. Ursula took to riding at once, and was soon allowed to have her own pony, but at my first lesson I was thrown; my pony jumped over me as I lay on the ground, and took a large piece out of my breeches and a slightly smaller piece out of my behind. I have never willingly been on a horse since. Mr Pringle tried to comfort me by

49

saying in his enchanting brogue, 'Miss Mary is no good on a horse but she's an artiste on a bicycle'; and, indeed, I infinitely preferred pretending that my bicycle (also passed down from Barbie) was a black thoroughbred.

Mr Pringle brought a Scotch element into our lives. Ursula was given a Decca gramophone for her birthday and all the Harry Lauder records. Nanny made herself a tartan kilt out of some plaid bought in the town and would dress up most evenings after high tea and reduce us to fits of giggles with her Harry Lauder imitations.

Soon after we got to Stretton, Robert gave me a copy of *Lavengro*. It was the first book after *The Tale of Mr Tod* that I remember reading to myself. I still could not read with ease but I persevered because I was so enthralled by it. Its atmosphere was so perfectly in accord with Carding Mill Valley, and out of them both a hero was born to me – Dicon a'Dale, vagabond, adventurer, self-declared outlaw, a rebel but not a thief, friend of gypsies, superb horseman, gambler, poet, flute-player and possessor of a miraculous power over all animals – who served me, with some additions and variations, for the rest of the time I was there. No hero I have ever read of in fiction or in history has matched the fascination of my Dicon with his straight black hair (from his Italian mother) and blue eyes (from his Irish father; he was, of course, an orphan), his wonderful courage and resourcefulness, his knowledge of strange medicines and brilliant linguistic powers. (He could understand the language of the birds as well as every other language under the sun.) The only weakness I allowed him was bad luck at gambling, so that he was always broke, though naturally, being a hero, generous to a fault. He was dressed in leather breeches, a red plush waistcoat and a brown corduroy coat with a silk handkerchief round his neck, and he always carried a cherrywood sword-stick with a silver mount. (Have I forgotten to say that he was an expert swordsman and was constantly fighting duels?) I had such a stick myself, though it did not contain a sword. I had picked it up one day in the road and kept it. The smell of cherrywood, even in imagination, brings back to me all the magic of Dicon.

The next book I read to myself was *Richard Carvel*, which

50

definitely placed Dicon in the eighteenth century. Gradually he gathered round him a band of young rebels who would die at a word from him and whom he sent out on various thrilling adventures – crossing great rivers (I jumped the brook); fleeing from the law (I pedalled my bicycle until my legs ached); swimming over to France on a moonless night (I swam round and round the bathing pool with one foot on the bottom); disposing of inconvenient corpses (I gingerly prodded a dead sheep I had found half in and half out of the stream).

Another book that greatly influenced me at this time was *The Silver Lattice*, an anthology of verse for children. It was full of enthralling pictures – *Flora Macdonald's Introduction to Prince Charlie*, *The Horse Fair* (where Dicon spent much of his time), *Swift and Stella*, *My Lady Rides*, *The North-West Passage*, *The Boyhood of Raleigh* (not so well reproduced as our nursery version), and, my particular favourite, *The Order of Release*, which, in spite of its title, I always took to be a betrayal. As I never bothered to find out who had painted the pictures I loved, it was not until I grew up that I discovered how much delight I owed to Millais. My favourite poems in the book, which I learnt by heart, were *The Swan's Nest*, *Sir Patrick Spens*, *How They Brought the Good News from Ghent to Aix*, *The Glove and the Lions* and *Letty's Globe*.

I never wanted to leave my valley for an instant. If a picnic to the Caradoc was suggested, or an excursion to Ludlow Castle, or to Shrewsbury because it was market day, I would not be of the party. The others could go without me, which they usually did, knowing I was perfectly safe alone in my valley.

As in London, lessons were my only bugbear. My diary put it dramatically: 'A shade of darkness fell over the valey as I woke up, I seemed to have grone older, my lims were stif. I had the sensation it was Monday and the week-end was over. Monday is allways a horid day for people who have lesons one feels as if you dont have a holiday for a nother *five* days.'

At first we used to bicycle into the town every morning to attend a small school. ('I had first prayers then scriptur then Eritimatik. We were asked our homework then Tables then signaling then Grammar for a quarter of an hour'), but we were soon taken away, I think because the headmistress objected to our wearing breeches. Or perhaps I was expelled. (I have an indistinct but pleasant recollection of sitting on top of a small boy and pummelling him with my fists as hard as I could.) Thereafter Ursula went daily to a crammer, a clergyman called Mr Woolley, who coached boys for Sandhurst (she was the only girl there), while I did lessons with a charming young lady, Miss Horne, who lived with her mother in a large white house just outside the town and no doubt needed some extra pocket-money. I never got the impression that she was qualified to teach, perhaps because she was so pleasantly easy-going and was obviously as bored by teaching me as I was by being taught, but we got on very comfortably together, for she was always willing to let me off a few minutes early. I suspect that she kept her watch fast on purpose. But she did manage to stimulate in me an interest in one period of history. This was Grattan's Parliament and the Irish troubles, maybe because it was the only period she knew, or perhaps because it was a period she wanted to learn about.

I took the United Irishmen to my heart, for they fitted perfectly into my own story. It was the right period; Dicon was anyway half-Irish and Mother had sung to us *The Wearing of the Green* for as long as I could remember. Besides, I too was almost half-Irish and very proud of it. Father's mother and Mother's grandmother had both been pure Irish. Dicon became a member of the Society and a close friend of Edward Fitzgerald, Napper Tandy, Hamilton Rowan, Wolfe Tone and the rest. (What magic names!) When I had a fall off my bicycle and hurt my knee so badly that I had to lay up for a week, I was very happy being Dicon after a duel, convalescing with the Fitzgeralds at Black Rock, waited on by the beautiful Pamela herself and by Edward's negro servant, Toby. While I was imagining, I would hold a piece of paper to the fire to turn it into parchment on which to write a code message sealed with a drop of blood from my own finger, which I would later bury under a stone next to the dead sheep.

The details I amassed about the United Irishmen must have come from Miss Horne, for we had no reference books. I could not learn enough about them, but her other lessons were as dull as those of any other governess. One morning she set me to write an essay on what I would do if my grandmother died and left me fifty pounds. I remember thinking it a particularly stupid subject and was deeply bored as I laboriously filled the requisite page and a half, but Miss Horne evidently found my effort amusing, for she sent it to Mother. Ursula showed it to Father, who was delighted with it and in his turn passed it on to his great friend, E. V. Lucas. He got it published in *Punch* under the name of Mary Landseer, and also included it in a book of his own, *Verena in the Midst*. I was at first outraged at having my serious composition laughed at, but when I saw it in print I became puffed up with pride. I give it here as a good example of the unthinking ruthlessness of childhood.

One day, I think it was the happiest day in the world for me. My grandmother died and left me £50. Without waiting to mourn or wait for her funeral I was walking along Oxford Street in surch of things to buy. My heart was as light as a feather as I walked and my boots were up in the ere.

First I thought what my husband would like me to have, then with a sudden thought I turned my steps home-would, and that night I went to a play, the next a nother, and so I went on until I had only 10*s* left. Then how I wished my other grandmother was died, but it was no good. And when I had children I wished I had not been so rash as to spend it on abusements, but had saved it, but it was gone for ever and my other grandmother never died, to my great misfortune.

Mother paid us occasional visits while we were at Stretton and would read aloud to us, but I found that I no longer wanted to be read to. I was afraid of spoiling Dicon by some contradictory imaginative impulse. *Lorna Doone*, *Kidnapped* and *Johnny Ludlow* could be fitted into Dicon's adventures, but there was just no place for *Dracula*. A whole day was ruined in trying somehow to fuse them together, but they refused to merge. Fortunately I was able to jettison *Dracula* the next day. If I were a child today I am sure I should be very unhappy with the constantly conflicting stimuli of films and television. My time at Stretton was so perfect just because there was no outside stimulus.

It was only Nitya's presence which was really distracting. He

53

was the one human being who had the power to dim my imaginative world, as the sun dims the fire. He and Krishna came twice to Stretton while we were there, staying both times at Miss Gamble's. The first visit was entirely happy and coincided with my tenth birthday. We were still in lodgings and I had an attic room (my first room to myself) with an uncovered skylight. I woke on my birthday morning to see the brilliant blue sky above me and was aware of a sudden intense rush of joy: 'I am alive; I am me.' And it was my birthday into the bargain, when I knew that everyone would take special pains to make me happy. It was the reverse of the mood which sometimes came over me, of wondering why there was a world at all — a mood of vast terror which came only at night, when even Nanny's presence in the bed next to me was no comfort, for might she not really be a witch disguised as Nanny?

My birthday presents were often a disappointment, for I had early acquired the habit of writing out showing-off birthday lists to astonish the grown-ups. They did not in the least represent my true wants, and invariably I was punished by being given what I had asked for. The only presents I remember from that tenth birthday were the ones Krishna and Nitya gave me — a silver knife on a silver chain and a man's silk scarf from Liberty's of a Paisley design on a dark green ground (this was the scarf that Dicon wore thereafter round his neck). I can still almost *smell* the happiness those presents gave me.

Their next visit was in the winter after we moved to Holly Cottage and there was snow on the ground. But this visit was entirely spoilt by Annie telling me on the morning after their arrival, just as we were about to set off up the valley to join them at Miss Gamble's, that I must have a dose that night because my breath was bad. We spent the whole day with them, tobogganing or sailing pieces of wood down the stream, and what a happy day it might have been if I had dared to open my mouth. As I never spoke very much anyway, I do not suppose anyone noticed my silence, and I am sure I had nothing to say, but I was acutely unhappy, scarcely able to breathe, my lips pressed tightly together; afraid too that a noxious stench might come down my nostrils if I let air out of them. For the most part I kept my woolly scarf round my nose and mouth and almost suffocated. If it had not been for my longing to be with Nitya, I should have happily used my affliction as an excuse for staying by myself. No doubt 'the boys' stayed on for a week or so, but I can remember nothing of their visit beyond that first miserable day.

Not even the Armistice took me out of my private world. (The bonfires were secret signals from Dicon to some of his band.) But there was one drama in the town – a real-life murder – which did succeed in invading my imagination. The small grocer we patronised in Church Stretton owned his own shop and was a charming old man with white hair and a pepper-and-salt moustache who served us with a gentle courtesy. I was devoted to him. Behind the counter, next to him, sat his wife, huddled in shawls. She was paralysed and an idiot and so dreadful in appearance that I dared not look at her. She always sat near the window so that she could look out. She had been like that for years, and people marvelled at the old man's cheerfulness and wonderful kindness to her. He carried her up and down stairs every day and did everything for her. Nanny said that she was as helpless as a baby. And then one night he killed her by dropping her out of the bedroom window. I was so upset that I could not imagine for a whole day. But the story had a happy ending. He was sentenced to life imprisonment, and in prison was allowed to hand out the groceries. I pictured him behind a counter exactly like his own, serving his fellow-prisoners with the same gentle smile but without the awful bundle in the shawls constantly beside him.

Although I never wanted the companionship of other children and was much happier playing alone, I did make one friend of my own age while we were at Stretton – a boy called Dan. He went to a boarding school in Shrewsbury but we sometimes played together in the holidays. We would catch trout with our hands – quite large trout, which lurked under the overhanging grassy banks of the stream; and when we had caught about half a dozen we would take them to his house in a bucket and empty them into the bath while we had tea. After tea we would play with them a little and then take them back in the bucket and release them into the stream. We must have caught the same fish over and over again, and in the end it became so easy to get hold of them that I was tempted to believe they came to know us and to enjoy their excursions.

Although I liked Dan as much as I could like any child, my heart used to sink when he appeared at the door to ask me to come and play with him. Nevertheless I told myself in a matter-of-fact way that I would probably marry him when I grew up. At the end of July 1919, when the dreadful day came to leave Stretton, Dan came to see me off. He appeared just as the train was about to start, awkwardly pushed a book into my hands, and then fled before I had time to thank him. It was a leather-bound copy of *The Cloister and the Hearth*. I have never seen him or heard of him since.

CHAPTER EIGHT

We spent those summer holidays of 1919 at Thorpeness, in Suffolk, where, as well as a sandy beach strewn with cornelians, there was a lake, in no place more than three feet deep, dotted with islands, on which children could take out sailing dinghies by themselves and learn to sail by trial and error. I had my eleventh birthday while we were there and Barbie came of age. As well as a number of Barbie's friends who stayed with us at our rented villa there were other friends of hers who had taken houses by the sea or along the lake shore, and there were dozens of children. We went about in gangs and there always seemed to be a party of some kind going on; but the greatest fun was going into Aldeburgh, as we did once a week for a serial film with Pearl White in it. One of Barbie's friends had a sports car and we children were piled into the dickey.

The gaiety of Barbie's life communicated itself even to me, and I came quite a way out of my shell and joined in the communal activities with almost my whole mind. The gramophone played continuously in our small house and the tunes which bring back to me that summer most nostalgically are *Smiles, On the Level You're a Little Devil, Till the Clouds Roll By* and *I Found a Rose in the Devil's Garden.* Nitya did not come to Thorpeness and I fell in love with one of Barbie's young men.

Lord Sandwich was also staying there, and when one day he lost his wife's wedding ring in the sand, I was lucky enough to find it. In the first flush of his gratitude he offered to give me anything I liked to ask for as a reward. Egged on by Nanny I asked for a bicycle, but was punished for my greed by receiving, after a delay of some weeks, a book called *Humphrey Bold.* Nanny's indignation was far greater than mine.

When we got back to London at the end of September it

was to a new house, 13 Mansfield Street, near Cavendish Square. Bedford Square had been sold at the end of the war, and while we were still at Stretton the rest of the family had been living in furnished houses, but now the new house was ready for us. Although the rooms were even larger than at Bedford Square there was less accommodation upstairs, so we were given as our nursery the former billiard-room on the ground floor at the back of the house looking on to a mews. This was a huge room with a parquet floor and a dais at one end. Above the billiard-room was a small racquet court. The large front drawing-room had been done up by Father with black walls, an emerald-green painted floor, black horsehair chair and sofa covers and canary-yellow curtains. He loved this house as much as he had disliked Bedford Square.

The term had not yet started when we moved in and Betty was still with us. It had always been one of her passions to make secret houses for herself, and she quickly made a house inside the cistern cupboard in the gentlemen's cloak-room next to the nursery, from which she could spy out on any unsuspecting gentlemen who came to dinner. When anything was missing we knew that Betty had taken it to beautify her house. When she was in a particularly friendly mood she would invite me up there. We had to go up by a ladder which we then pulled up after us, and we were always obliged to keep a crack of the door open to enable us to see, for we were not allowed to have a candle up there, but she made it wonderfully snug with rugs, cushions and pictures.

She and I had both been given scooters for our last birthdays and for the first few days after our arrival at Mansfield Street we scooted back and forth from the nursery to the front door leaving dirty tracks on the black-and-white marble paving of the hall, and shouting, 'Look out, look out,' at the top of our voices. We must have been dreadfully tiresome, but I know that my own whoops, though they may have sounded high-spirited, were in reality cries of protest at being removed from my beloved valley. The gaiety at Thorpeness had not been suitable for Dicon, and I was not surprised that he did not come to me there, but I had hoped to recapture him as soon as we got back to the comparative peace of London. Alas, he did not come, and I missed him grievously. I fell back on playing with toys again, and, now that we had a parquet floor, dancing to the gramophone. I danced mostly by myself or with a cushion for a partner, but Ursula and I would sometimes dance together, our favourite duet being one she had invented called The Lackadaisical Prince and the Spirit of Evil. For this we dressed up (we had a large trunk full of dressing-up clothes), Ursula in orange chiffon as the Spirit of Evil, and I in a pale blue satin suit with a lace jabot.

We had always spent occasional week-ends with Mother's mother, the Dowager Lady Lytton, at Homewood, the house at Knebworth which Father had designed for her, and the first time we went there after our return from Thorpeness, Dicon came back to me. A couple of miles from the house is a wild common called Rabley Heath, and as I walked there alone on the first morning, Dicon suddenly appeared. I realised then that he belonged to the heath and the moors and the wild hills and valleys. I discovered that he had Romany blood in his veins. His Italian mother, although the daughter of a duke (for Dicon was an aristocrat to his finger-tips), had been half-gypsy. I was immensely relieved to discover this because it explained his strange aversion to towns. Nevertheless I could hardly bear to go back to Homewood for lunch in case I lost him again, but fortunately I was to find that for the next eighteen months he always came to me on Rabley Heath.

We usually spent Easter at Homewood, so it is connected in my mind with the first birds' nests and the first hot days when we would shed our clothes while playing in the garden. First our woolly coats and shoes and stockings would come off; then our bloomers and finally our vests, to lie in little pools on the grass tennis-court until Annie came along to pick them up. (The tennis-court had been given over to the sole care of a goat in the war and it never recovered.) Nothing gave me a greater sense of freedom and well-being than to run about with only a cotton dress and a pair of knickers on, and to feel the grass under my bare toes.

Staying at Homewood had its disadvantages, though. I was devoted to Granny and she was particularly fond of me because I was so 'peaceful' as she called it (and she liked my eyebrows. To her 'the brows' were a very important feature of a face), but as we had our meals with her we were obliged to behave particularly well, and we had to wait for breakfast until her accustomed hour. She always came down to breakfast but did not have it until nine o'clock. She sat with a silver jug of hot water on her lap at every meal to keep her hands warm. She had been a very great lady, Vicereine of India and the Ambassadress in Paris, and she kept her beautiful manners to the end of her long life. (She lived to be ninety-five.) When the Rector came to lunch on Sundays, the book of memoirs (her favourite reading) would be put out of sight and a religious work substituted. She already seemed to belong to history. She pronounced cucumber, cowcumber; laundry, larndry; soot, sut; and blouse and vase, bloose and vaize. She sent her hair-combings to Paris to be made up into curls which her maid pinned to the front of her head. Although very much reduced in circumstances since her ambassadorial days, she never did her own hair. To fall below the standard of a personal maid would have been unthinkable. There was one bath in the house (Homewood had been built in 1901), green-tiled and encased in oak, but she never used it and continued to have a tin tub in her room until she died in 1936.

The furniture and pictures at Homewood were as familiar as our own at home. At the top of the broad staircase with its apple-green carpet, which I remembered from the days when I could climb it only by bringing one foot up to the other, was a life-size picture by Millais of Granny's adored dead husband – Mother's father, our 'Gam-gam' – in a beard and frock-coat. I did not feel at all drawn to him. In the drawing-room over the writing-table were small portraits of Granny's father and mother, Edward and Elizabeth Villiers. Edward Villiers had died of consumption at the age of forty-three. I was said to look like him in this picture – or rather, as I put it to myself, he looked like me. The resemblance was a very flattering one to *me*, and whenever I was in the drawing-room I would spend most of my time gazing at him. I was far more interested in him than in any of my other forebears. As we looked alike I felt there must be some special kinship between us stronger than mere blood. In his picture he appeared happy enough, with a round, gentle, girlish face, framed in soft wavy hair, and yet I had been told that all his life he suffered from terrible bouts of melancholia and almost ceaseless abdominal pain which made him dreadfully irritable. He was convinced that all his abdominal organs were diseased, and left instructions that a post-mortem be carried out. He believed that this would vindicate him: far from being a hypochondriac it would be discovered that he had borne his agonising complaint with the most amazing fortitude. The post-mortem was duly carried out but nothing was found to be wrong with him beyond his diseased lungs. This story haunted me. I could not bear him not to be vindicated. Surely the doctor who had carried out the post-mortem had not been thorough enough. I refused to believe that there had been nothing wrong with him. In the eyes of his great-granddaughter at least he was wholly exonerated.

Granny expected me to play piquet with her in the evenings, which bored me very much. She cheated shamelessly, and, like most grown-ups in my experience, she did not like to lose, so I had to let her win and this made the game even less interesting. Another great drawback to staying at Homewood was that she insisted on my going to church with her on Sundays. This had some slight compensation, however, as we went by horse-fly. I sat up on the box, and at least once during the journey the horse would lift his tail and do 'bigway' (I could not understand why this word was not in the dictionary) and I never ceased to marvel at his technique for doing it while he was trotting. He seemed to have no shame (perhaps because I could not see his face) and therefore I did not mind watching him.

But the greatest disadvantage of staying there was that Granny lived with her invalid daughter, Aunt Con, who was half-paralysed. Aunt Con had been a militant suffragette. She had been in prison three or four times and her health had been ruined by forcible feeding. Betty got on splendidly with Aunt Con, who was very musical and encouraged her in her early efforts at composition, but to me she was wholly terrifying. I was frightened enough of her when she was shuffling about downstairs doing exquisite Japanese flower

61

decorations with her left hand (it was her right side which was paralysed), but much worse was when we had to visit her, each in turn, in her very hot bedroom where she lay in bed peeling grapes for her Pekinese. She always wore purple velvet, even in bed, with her suffragette medals pinned to her chest, and she had flannel sheets which made the room feel horribly stuffy; but more dreadful than anything, she expected me to sit on a chair and converse with her. I was at ease only sitting on the floor and I could not make conversation.

I have since discovered what a wonderful person she was, and one of my deepest regrets is that I failed to value her. I wonder why it was. She was always gentle, a quality which children appreciate, and she should have appealed to me particularly because she was pernickety in her cleanliness and tidiness (her birthday treat as a child was to clean out the lavatory, and every copper that came into her possession she polished until it shone), but most children shy away from illness and from seeing grown-ups undressed or in bed. I once had the dreadful experience of seeing Father in the bath. It was during the only visit he paid us at Church Stretton. He had forgotten to lock the door and I barged in to find him lying in the bath, happily relaxed, with an enormous sponge between his legs. I quickly withdrew, shocked almost to tears. I had heard there was a difference in anatomy between men and women, and for years after this I was not sure that this difference was not a huge growth of sponge.

CHAPTER NINE

In the autumn of that year, 1919, Ursula and I were sent to Queen's College in Harley Street, simply because it was so close to Mansfield Street that we could go there by ourselves. Without telling me, Ursula pretended to be a Jew in order to get off prayers, and I was very startled one day when someone asked me why my sister was a Jew and I was not, and furious that she had not shared with me this rewarding subterfuge. But Ursula stayed only one or two terms at Queen's and then went on to a fashionable London finishing school, Miss Wolff's, in South Audley Street, where Barbie had been for a while. Mother had suffered very much as a child from never being allowed to go about by herself and was consequently determined to give her children greater freedom. She had allowed Barbie to go to Miss Wolff's alone, but Barbie, in her turn, suffered from being the only girl there who was not escorted by a maid. She used to wait behind the others after the last class, pretending that her maid was always late in coming to fetch her.

I remained at Queen's for four years, first in the School and then in the College. When I had been there about three years I was very hurt one day when Father asked me what school I was at. As far as I know he never took the slightest interest in my education.

Betty left her boarding school at the end of 1919 and joined Ursula at Miss Wolff's. Thereafter she gave weekly *thés dansants* in our nursery, exclusively for girls, which she allowed me to attend.

The term must already have started when Mother took me round to Queen's College for the first time, for when I was shown over the classrooms by Miss Lewer, the headmistress, the girls were all at their lessons. Miss Lewer paused in the

63

door of one classroom and told me that this was probably the form I should be in. I was then set down to do a simple entrance examination, which consisted in part of some sums in long division; but these I was unable even to attempt. As a result of this test I was placed two forms lower than the class which had been pointed out to me.

This humiliating experience – I was far larger as well as older than any girl in my class – stimulated my scholastic ambition. I began to work competitively and perhaps for that very reason to enjoy school; but I was so slow that to catch up I was obliged to spend far more time over my homework than I should have done. (There was to be no more reading aloud after tea.) I was too excited to eat any breakfast before starting off, and even the vegetarian parts of the lunch at school, the vegetables and pudding which were all I was obliged to eat, were so disgusting that I used to wrap them in pages of an exercise book and put them down the lavatory; but Nanny would provide me with Russian salad from Selfridge's for nursery tea (how delicious it was), and this became my only weekday meal. I lost my baby-fat while developing a bust which I stooped to hide, and went proudly into black woollen stockings, a gym dress and school tie. My only triumph that first term came when one day we were told to learn by heart a poem of our choosing as homework and recite it in class next day. I recited the whole of *The Swan's Nest*, without disclosing that I knew it already, while all the other girls chose the shortest possible poems.

I used to get home most days at about four, and as I opened the front door (I had my own latchkey, worn, with my school locker-key, on a black cord round my neck), I would look at once to see whether 'the boys'' pale grey Homburg hats and gold-headed canes were on the hall-table. They were both living in London when we first moved to Mansfield Street and came to our house more than ever before. If the table was bare a bleak dejection descended on me, but if the magic hats and sticks were there I skipped along to the nursery with an uprush of joy and vitality. They would be up in the back drawing-room with Mother, and I would have to start my homework before tea. I would leave the nursery door open, however, and if I heard them coming downstairs I would go along to the hall on some pretext and pretend I had run into them by chance. Sometimes they left without my knowing, but the disappointment of that was no worse than seeing the front door close behind them, for at best I saw them only for a few moments in the hall. As long as I knew they were in the house I was happy.

As I grew older my love made me shyer than ever of Nitya, and the joy I felt in his presence hardly made up for the desolation of his going away. I still have a tiny note-book in which I wrote that autumn: 'Oh, I have a secrit wich know one nows. It is awful my secrit. It weys upon me like a weight. It pounds me, it hurts me, and if one person was not on this [earth?] I would not have such a great secrit.' I remember writing that and feeling that my love was too big to be contained within myself, and consequently being terrified that I might give away my secret.

Occasionally 'the boys' would come and have tea with us in the nursery, and at week-ends I would go up to the drawing-room to see them. I had now been promoted to dining-room lunch on Sundays, when they would often be there. Krishna had just discovered P. G. Wodehouse and Leacock and would read *Piccadilly Jim* and *Nonsense Novels* aloud to us, laughing so much that he spluttered over the words. And then occasionally on a Saturday we would go with them to a cinema after tea, either to the New Gallery or to the London Pavilion. (We saw at least two Sessue Hayakawa films with them. He was by far my favourite film star because of his brown skin and glossy black hair, so like Nitya's, and I was deeply incensed that he was never allowed to marry the heroine in the end. He always had to sacrifice himself.) There was no greater happiness for me than these outings, not because of the rare pleasure of going to a cinema but because it meant a longer time than usual in Nitya's company. It was a matter of chance whether I sat next to him or not (I was quite incapable of manoeuvring it), but when I did I hardly saw what was happening on the screen, so acutely receptive was I to his physical closeness. I felt I had mouths all over my body drinking him in.

But there was one such promised treat that I entirely ruined for myself. We were all in the nursery, just preparing to set out, when I suddenly complained of a pain in my stomach. I was losing the purity of my love, in that I wanted some return, if only to be noticed as a nuisance. The result of this bid to draw attention to myself was that the others went off without me while Sir Bruce Bruce-Porter, our family doctor, was sent for. When he came he felt about for an inflamed appendix but, of course, could find nothing because my pain was entirely imaginary. I shall never forget my misery as I lay on the nursery sofa with Nanny fussing over me, a victim of my own showing off.

It was on another occasion when the boys were ragging with us in the nursery that Nitya, thowing himself back into a chair with one leg over the arm, made a small black mark with his shoe on the white-washed wall just on the left of the fireplace. This mark was all I had of him when he was not there, and it became a kind of fetish for me. Every evening before going to bed I had to kiss it three times, and three times touch it with the kissed tips of my fingers. It was not always easy to get the nursery to myself to carry out this secret observance, and often I had to come down after everybody was in bed, and once or twice when I forgot, I had to get out of my warm bed in the middle of the night and creep downstairs – but for years (I am not exaggerating) I never missed a single day in carrying out this ritual when we were in London. I hoped that my reward would be Nitya's love one day. I knew he would never love me without supernatural intervention.

CHAPTER TEN

Krishna went to live in Paris in January 1920. He had failed in all his examinations for London University and it was now thought best by the powers who ruled his life that he should learn French, if nothing else. Nitya meanwhile moved into another flat on his own and began to study for the Bar.

Ursula and I both had measles that winter. She had them first and I was fully expecting to catch them, so when one morning I found that my imagination could not work magic on my toys, I recognised that I was ill and went about the nursery deliberately collecting such playthings as I might need in bed when I was better.

Nitya, I knew, had taken Ursula for her first convalescent walk along Portland Place, and I hoped I might receive the same treatment; but, alas, it was Nanny who took me out for the first time. I never walked with Nitya along Portland Place, although for years it was a dream of mine to do so.

In March Nitya left England with the intention of going to India. An older Indian friend of his and Krishna's, Ratansi Moraji, who was a cotton-merchant in Bombay, came to England on a visit and Nitya decided to go back with him. Nitya came to Mansfield Street with Ratansi one afternoon in Ratansi's car to say goodbye, when only I was at home. I happened to be in the hall when the parlourmaid opened the door, for I was just going out to post a letter. Nitya was on the doorstep while Ratansi remained in the car. Nitya asked for Ursula and I came shyly forward with a beating heart. I could sense his disappointment at finding only me at home. He handed me a big box of chocolates from Charbonnel & Walker which he had brought for us all as a goodbye present. He did not suggest waiting until the others came back and I was too shy to ask him to stay. As he got into the car I ran out

67

to post my letter in the box at the corner, giving a little wave over my shoulder which I hoped would look gay and carefree, while all the time I felt I was bursting with grief. How long would it be before I saw him again? It might be months and months. I was glad that I happened to wearing my best day-dress – a navy-blue stockinet passed down from Ursula (I am not sure that it had not originally belonged to Barbie) with a wide band of moleskin at the bottom and a narrower band round the V-neck. I had coveted that dress ever since Ursula first had it, and had jealously watched her wearing it, knowing that one day it would be mine. When I got back into the house I noticed a great split in the moleskin band at the bottom. This seemed to me symbolic of what had happened to my heart as I ran to post my letter, and I never cared for the dress again.

For the first time in my life I had an impulse to be polite. I wanted to write to Nitya to thank him for the chocolates but I did not know his address.

Nitya did not go to India after all. He got only as far as Paris when he received a cable from Mrs Besant from India telling him not to come. Recently I have seen one of Krishna's letters to Mother written at this date from Paris, saying how miserable Nitya was at having his plans cancelled at the last moment. He had 'burnt his boats' in London, had spent a great deal of money, and did not now know what to do with himself. He finally went to the South of France for a while with Ratansi and then returned to England at the beginning of May. He was back in time for Barbie's wedding.

In March Barbie had become engaged to Euan Wallace. She had told us one day that she had a friend coming to see her the next afternoon who had something very important to say to her, and would we please keep out of the way. I was on the watch next afternoon from the bedroom landing and saw the parlourmaid coming upstairs to the drawing-room followed by a tall dark man with a black moustache. Either that evening or the next morning Barbie told us she was engaged. I was dreadfully puzzled as to how she could have known that he was going to propose to her.

She was married on May 10 at the Savoy Chapel, attended by six bridesmaids including Ursula, Betty and me. The other three were Hermione and Davina Lytton and another first cousin, Kathleen Balfour. I was paired with Betty, and as I came up the aisle I passed Nitya (I was looking out for him) sitting on the outside of the pew, so close that I could easily have touched him. His pale grey hat, which meant so much to me from looking for it on the hall-table every afternoon when I got back from school, was on his knees and both his hands rested on the gold knob of his cane. I knew he had loved Barbie. (Did I know this intuitively or had I heard it? I cannot be sure.) Did he still love her? What was he feeling? Was he very unhappy? If so I longed to console him. I tried to send out waves of loving comfort to him during the ceremony. I thought of nothing else. For the first time I wanted to sacrifice myself, to do something for somebody else even if it made me unhappy.

The wedding was in the morning and afterwards there was a lunch party at Mansfield Street, About a dozen small round tables had been set up in the dining-room. I had taken it for granted that Nitya would be coming to this lunch and had consequently been greatly looking forward to the wedding. My disappointment therefore was acute when I found that he had not been invited, or so I supposed, for he did not come. When I saw the tables fill up and no Nitya I nearly cried. I could not understand how Barbie had failed to invite him, but then I could not understand either how she could have married anyone else when Nitya loved her. I had no jealousy of her. She was so beautiful that it seemed only natural that everyone should love her, but I did feel angry with her that day because I was sure she had hurt Nitya.

That summer Ratansi came to London again and was extraordinarily kind to Betty and me. He took us out several times in his grand motor car, the joy of these trips for me being that Nitya always came with us. There was one unfor-gettable day, June 19, when we went to Ranelagh with Ratansi in the afternoon, out to dinner with him and then on to a theatre in a box. I must have been in Nitya's company for something like eight hours on end, and the intensity of my emotion for all that time was so exhausting that I was almost glad when the evening was over. My Ranelagh ticket became another relic to be kissed three times every evening, and better than the mark on the wall it could be taken with me wherever I went. I still have it, not that I have deliberately kept it, but it has never got lost – a round piece of green pasteboard, about the size of a half crown, smeared with a drop of blood from my finger to make the magic more potent. Its reliquary, where it still resides, is a small purse of mauve brocade.

That same summer Nitya came down for a day to Homewood where we were staying – or it may have been in the spring. Anyway, it was a perfect hot day and he and Ursula and I lay out on the grass in the afternoon. When we got up I marked in my mind the spot where the grass had been crushed by his body. I knew it ever afterwards, though no eyes but mine could have seen his invisible shape impressed there. It was hallowed ground. I visited it often, but never walked on it, though I sometimes knelt down to kiss it.

In November of the same year, 1920, Robert, who was only nineteen, made a runaway marriage to Scotland. This was a great excitement for us. Detectives came to the house because Father was anxious to track him down and stop the wedding. I longed to lie for Robert, but even more to be brought into court and commit perjury for him. Perjury, I knew, was something you committed when you loved a person more than truth and honour, and I would have been ashamed of any love which did not go to those lengths. Naturally I was on the side of romance and could not understand Father's apparent harshness.

As a result of Robert's marriage I understood that we three girls who were left were made Wards of Court.* I had no idea what this meant but I felt greatly privileged by it and set apart. Already I was set apart at school because that summer, while I was still only eleven, I had become what I looked upon as a woman. By the autumn I had caught up at school, and was now, after a year, in the proper class for my age, and very gratified at being the only girl in that class to be periodically excused drill.

I liked being different. One of my favourite daydreams was to be sent for by Miss Lewer and told that both my parents

*Mother also had this impression, and certainly believed it to be a fact, but I think now that it can only have been a threat.

70

had been killed in an accident. What appealed to me particularly about this piece of imagining was the brave way in which I faced the class afterwards when they all knew of my great affliction. ('Do you know, she didn't shed a single tear! Wasn't she wonderful?') I do not think this shows any abnormal heartlessness. I was deeply distressed if ever I heard a cross word between Mother and Father, which was extremely rare, and I was miserable when Mother had one of her frequent headaches. If one sometimes imagined the glory of being an orphan, one imagined no less often the pleasure of punishing one's parents because they did not love one enough. Ursula and I ran away from Mansfield Street one day when we felt for some reason that we were not sufficiently appreciated. We wandered about the streets for what seemed to us hours, and then, relenting, and feeling some compunction at the grief we must have caused, returned home, only to find that we had not even been missed.

CHAPTER ELEVEN

In February of the next year, 1921, Nitya had chicken-pox very badly. He took no proper care of himself after this illness. He was living on his own, eating too little and working too hard. In May, when he had been with us to the New Gallery Cinema one afternoon, he suddenly coughed and brought up blood. It was the first intimation that he had tuberculosis.

Mother wrote to tell Krishna, who immediately sent for Nitya to join him in Paris where he was still living. In Paris Krishna had become very friendly with a Madame de Manziarly and her family of three daughters and a son. Nitya had also made great friends with this family the year before when he had stayed in Paris on his way to the South of France, and he and Krishna had spent the previous September with them at Amphion on the Lake of Geneva. Madame de Manziarly was Russian and a Theosophist, married to a Frenchman who died that year. She had great faith in a certain Dr Carton who claimed to be able to cure all diseases by diet, and it was arranged that he should treat Nitya. Dr Carton lived at Boissy St Leger, about ten miles from Paris, and Madame de Manziarly took a house for Nitya at Boissy so that he might be near this doctor.

To my intense joy Mother took Betty and me over to Boissy for the summer holidays, renting a house close to the one where Nitya was staying with Krishna, Madame de Manziarly and the youngest Manziarly girl, Yolande, who was about fifteen. The middle daughter, Marcelle, and a young Indian Theosophist, Rajagopal, who had been sent over by Mrs Besant to go to Cambridge and had made friends with Nitya in London, stayed with us.

Our house was extremely primitive. There was an inside

water closet but it smelt so badly that we used to stand outside and pray for the one who was in there. We had our baths in a tin tub under a weeping willow in the garden, and the garden itself was a jungle containing an empty sunk tank which had once been a swimming pool; but on the credit side our French cook made the best fried potatoes I have ever eaten.

Krishna spent most of the day with us and we played games, such as Blind Man's Bluff, Statues and Russian Whispering, in the empty swimming pool, or we would all go into the adjoining fields and play rounders – all except Madame de Manziarly, that is, and Nitya who was leading an invalid life. But Mother would join in these games with her whole heart. Krishna was now twenty-five but he had retained his sense of fun. There was no one better to play games or laugh with.

It was an intensely hot summer and I slept in an attic, whose white walls were so thickly covered with the bloody corpses of mosquitoes that they seemed to be hung with rosebud-patterned wallpaper. Every evening before going to bed I would add to the carnage with my bedroom slipper, but even so there was not a part of me, left uncovered by the sheet, which was not badly bitten – worst of all my eyelids which were permanently swollen. It never occurred to me or to anyone else that I might sleep under a net. But in spite of this persecution I was extraordinarily happy during those weeks at Boissy, with a happiness different from anything I had ever known before. I was really more elated than happy. Perhaps the mosquitoes had given me a fever or maybe it was the heat that had brought me suddenly into flower. I had never known such a heat and I revelled in it. There was a café across the road from our house, and night and day two tunes came jingling across to us from an electric barrel-organ – *C'est Mon Homme* and *J'en ai Marre* – which greatly stimulated the erotic side of my nature. I felt full of an astonishing power to attract, which considering my puffy eyelids and blotched face seems rather ludicrous.

I did not see Nitya more than three or four times while we were there, but every day I had the hope of seeing him. Moreover I was perhaps even more in love with love that summer than with him. There was an intoxicating climate of

73

in-loveness around me; there was magic in those hot nights when we sat in the moonlight on the concrete rim of the sunk basin playing childish whispering games while the erotic beat of those two tunes went on continually. They drove poor Betty almost mad but I never wanted them to stop.

Mother had met the Manziarlys before we came to Boissy, when she had once or twice been over to Paris to visit Krishna, but Betty and I were meeting them for the first time. The eldest daughter and the son were not with us but we had seen them in Paris on the way to Boissy. Madame de Manziarly, though small and rather plump, had a beautiful face with a perfect complexion – if she had been younger she would have been my ideal conception of the Madonna – but her passionately voiced convictions on every subject, and her vitality, were overwhelming to my British phlegm. I had never known such intensity.

The whole family abounded in charm, vitality, wit and gaiety, and, with their French outspokenness, were something fascinatingly new in my experience. It must indeed have been refreshing for Krishna to meet them in Paris, for before that ours was the only home he had ever known, and we were very prim and self-contained compared with the Manziarlys. They were delightful with Mother, calling her 'Maladi' and addressing her with many terms of endearment in their charming broken English, and under their affectionate badinage she blossomed out as I had never seen her. It was Marcelle who had started us praying outside the 'clo', as she called it, for she was as uninhibited about the functions of nature as about everything else. She was a wonderful tonic to me and I grew greatly to love the whole family when once my shyness of their forthrightness had worn off. We were so English and they were so French, yet we played equivalent roles in Krishna's life. It must have been pleasant for him to have two such totally different milieus as foster-homes. He had known us much longer, and perhaps felt more relaxed with us, but the Manziarlys must have been much more stimulating, and then, whereas Mother's whole life now was Theosophy, Madame de Manziarly had kept up her outside activities and was able to introduce him to interesting people and new worlds of thought, art and literature.

One hot afternoon, on one of the few occasions when we were up at Nitya's house and were all sitting in the garden grouped round him as he reclined in a basket-chair, Yo, as we always called Yolande, who had just washed her short hair and dried it in the sun, flopped down at his feet and inclining her head towards him invited him to feel how soft her hair was. This impressed me as a particularly charming and feminine gesture, but at the same time I marvelled at her self-confidence. Would I, who had known him so much longer than she, ever dare to make such an overture? And yet the fact that he put out his hand and felt her hair with evident pleasure made him seem somehow more accessible to me.

Another incident directly to do with Nitya that I recall from that summer was acting some kind of play or charade in front of him and him telling me afterwards that I was a born actress. This was the first personal remark he ever addressed to me as far as I know, and it made me extremely happy, not because he had praised my acting but because I felt that at last I had become an individual to him, someone in my own right, instead of merely the dull baby of the Lutyens family.

But after that summer I was not to see him or Krishna again for nearly two years. From Boissy they went to Montesano in Switzerland where Dr Rolier, a great specialist in tuberculosis, declared Nitya to be cured, and in November Mrs Besant sent for them to come to India. She considered that Krishna was now ready to take his acclaimed place in the Theosophical scheme as the body which the Lord would use when he came, and she wanted him to give one of the four public lectures at the Theosophical Convention to be held at Benares that winter. Nitya, now that he was cured, would naturally go with him. These two brothers were never happy when long apart, though I think it was Krishna who depended on Nitya more than the other way round. While they were separated merely by the English Channel there had been constant trips back and forth, but now it was unthinkable that Nitya should be left behind. The idea of his making a career as a barrister was never seriously considered, I think, even before he lost his health. The

Theosophical work must always come first, and it was made quite clear to both boys that they were expected to repay the money spent on their education in service to the Society.

Mother went with Father to India that winter (I knew she was really only following Krishna) and was away for three months. (It was on the occasion of this, their first visit to India together, that Father sent us a telegram from Marseilles saying: 'Pa and Ma sails'.) When she returned to England in March 1922, the boys went off to Sydney where Charles Webster Leadbeater, the joint Protector with Mrs Besant of the Order of the Star, lived as the head of a community of young people whom he was training in the esoteric teachings of Theosophy. It was Leadbeater who had first 'discovered' Krishna in 1909 at the Theosophical headquarters at Adyar near Madras, and who had been responsible for his early training. In 1913 he had gone to live in Sydney, and three years later had become a Bishop in the Liberal Catholic Church, a side-line of Theosophy.

In Sydney Nitya had a relapse, and as it was thought to be too hot for him to return by the Indian Ocean, he and Krishna went off to California where a house was lent to them in the Ojai Valley, seventeen hundred feet up, not far from Santa Barbara. Later this house was bought for them by a subscription raised by Mrs Besant. It was the first home of their own they had ever known.

Soon after they got to Ojai, Nitya, on the recommendation of some American friends, began to have treatment from a pupil of that Dr Abrams who had invented a machine which was said to diagnose and cure most diseases by electrical waves. He and Krishna made friends at this time with a Californian girl of nineteen called Rosalind. Krishna wrote to Mother to tell her about this girl; how they had got to know her while she was on a visit to some neighbours; how she came in every day to look after Nitya, and how devoted Nitya had become to her. Mother passed all this on to me without realising how much it hurt me, for I was still master of my secret. In due course a snapshot arrived of Krishna and Nitya with a tall, extremely pretty girl standing between them. I had never seen Nitya looking so happy, and for the first time I knew the hateful disquiet of jealousy.

That autumn in Ojai Krishna experienced a great spiritual revelation, which was to be the turning-point in his life. Until then he had only half-heartedly accepted his role as the coming World Teacher, but from this time he became sure of himself and his mission. Mother's excitement at what had happened communicated itself in some measure to me. Nitya also was profoundly changed by Krishna's experience.

Because of Nitya's health they stayed a whole year at Ojai, the longest they had ever been in one place, and it was not until June 1923 that they finally returned to England. It was now thought for the second time that Nitya was cured, although he was warned that he would have to be very careful.

CHAPTER TWELVE

My own life during the twenty-one months when I did not see Nitya was mostly taken up with school work. In the autumn after Boissy, when I was thirteen, I entered the College where we were taught for the most part by Cambridge professors. We felt very important at being called Miss So-and-So instead of by our Christian names. These male teachers were a great stimulus to work, not that my susceptible heart was ever remotely touched by any of them, but they gave us dignity and therefore a sense of responsibility. By overworking in the evenings, sometimes until after midnight, I managed some weeks to reach the top of my class, and for the same reason I did very well in exams, but I was always aware that had I been at a boarding school, with only a limited period for home-work, I should never have risen from the bottom. Over my essays in particular I used to spend hours. None of my school-friends knew how hard I really worked, for I played the clown at school. I found it a quick and easy way to popularity and a good cover for my real feelings. I had friends but no intimates.

At fourteen I became what was called a non-compounder – that is, I took only those subjects which interested me and dropped the rest. French and mathematics were the first to be jettisoned. This was done without Mother's approval (Father as I have already said took no interest in my schooling whatsoever), but neither did she disapprove. I do not think I even consulted her. She was too busy with her own concerns to worry about mine.

In the best tradition of girls' schools I fell in love with our very pretty games mistress, Miss Kershaw and got into the netball team so as to see more of her. To attract her attention I used to pretend to have fits after a hard game, when I would

gasp like an asthma sufferer, but she soon put a stop to this
nonsense by telling me that I would not be allowed to play at
all if I had so little stamina. Miss Kershaw also taught us
botany and again in a bid for her notice I would behave like a
delinquent moron in class only to come out top in the
end-of-term exam. This ruse succeeded better than the fits.
She really seemed puzzled by it and kept me back after class
on the day we broke up to tax me with the discrepancy. I am
sure she believed I had managed to cheat in some way.

It was also to get her to notice me that during one botany
lesson I cut the cane of some of the classroom chairs with a
pair of scissors. For this crime I was sent to the Principal,
Professor Edwards, who had a long red beard, taught mathematics to the Seniors, and was so grand that we never saw
him except at the Annual Gathering when the Bishop of
London came to give us a homily and Sir Philip Chetwode to
judge our drill display (he had some pretty harsh things to say
about it).

When I entered the Professor's study, where I had never
been before, and found him standing there in all his fiery-
bearded fierceness, I was trembling so much that I could
hardly stand and making up speeches in my head to tell him
how I would pay for the damage out of my own pocket-
money. He seemed almost equally uncomfortable and at a
loss where to begin, but after some hemming and hawing
started awkwardly, 'Now, let me see now. Miss Lutyens.
Lutyens. That name rings a bell. Didn't you have a relation
who was a great runner at Cambridge?'

It turned out to be Uncle Bill, Father's youngest brother,
though I had never heard until that moment that he was a
runner. He had saved me and I was grateful to him ever
afterwards. No mention was made of my crime and after a
pleasant chat about Uncle Bill I was dismissed. I do not think
that Father was even asked to pay for re-caning the chairs.

But the climax of my relationship with Miss Kershaw (if
anything so one-sided can be called a relationship) came when
I met her at tea one afternoon at the house of a fellow-
member of the netball team. She kissed this girl and her sister
when she arrived, and then, turning to me, said with a look of
great distaste, 'I suppose I shall have to kiss you too.' In spite

79

of her obvious reluctance to touch me I did not for several days wash my cheek where her lips had brushed me. I wonder whether she had the slightest inkling of my feelings for her. She left to get married soon after this and I have never been in love with a woman since.

But to go back for a moment to the Easter holidays when I was still thirteen. A great unhappiness came to me then while staying with Granny at Homewood. I set off by myself for Rabley Heath directly after breakfast on the first morning, looking forward to a long session in Dicon's company, only to find when I got there that I could not evoke him. I wandered about miserably for nearly two hours, but hard as I tried to keep my mind open to receive him it would keep filling up with dreary conjectures such as what I ought to do with myself in the future; whether I should take a commercial course at Queen's when the time came, and what subjects I should give up when I became a non-compounder in the autumn. Remembering the day when I was sickening for measles and my imagination had failed me, I finally went back to the house and asked Nanny to take my temperature, but, alas, I was not ill. I had simply, without warning, been cast out of the kingdom of my childhood. I suffered dreadfully from this rude deposition. I felt exiled, though in fact I suppose I was lucky to have been allowed to remain in that kingdom for almost two years after puberty.

For some years after this my imagination lay dormant, and when it did eventually start to function again it was trammelled by a conscience which impelled me to capture my stories in written words, thus curtailing their free roaming and linking them to the ardours of self-discipline.

But fortunately it was just at the time of my dispossession that the Doll's House which Father had designed for Queen Mary was being constructed in our drawing-room with the black walls. Furnishings of all sorts were arriving for it every day – linen, glass, china, books, pictures, curtains, chandeliers, wine-bottles, golf-clubs, motor-cars – as well as the fittings and furniture which Father had designed. I went into the drawing-room at all times to watch its progress and came to look upon it almost as my private possession. So much of the furniture was familiar to me. The bed in the Princess

Royal's room was a perfect miniature of the beds Father had designed for Barbie and Ursula; the chandelier in the nursery was a copy of the one he had made for Barbie's new nursery, while the kitchen cupboards were reproductions of our own. I realised that this was the house we would have lived in if Father had been rich enough to build it for himself. It was his own dream-house, and because I was imbued with his taste it was my dream-house too. It took no effort of imagination to see us living in it.

No wonder Father did not like coming away with us for holidays to the schools or rectories which Mother rented. We spent the summer holidays of 1922 in a school at Hemel Hempstead. I had a tea party for my birthday at which I must have been showing off as usual because Mother said very sharply to the assembled company, which included some school-friends who were staying with me, 'You can see Mary is still a baby although she is fourteen today.' This snub in front of my friends went to the quick. I could not remember another occasion in the whole of my life when Mother had snubbed me, but instead of being grateful for being spared so long, I was all the more resentful of this single snub which had spoiled my birthday – the one day of the year when I ought to be sure of being handled with kid gloves. When I went to bed that night I vowed I would never forgive her.

Was it being told that I was still a baby that urged me that summer to indulge in experimental kisses with a charming young man to the strains of *Avalon, The Japanese Sandman, Say it with Music* and *I'm Forever Blowing Bubbles*? I found that kissing was a most delightful occupation and that the feelings it produced linked up with sensations in the past which I had not realised had any connection with love-making. In other words I discovered for myself that I had had sexual feelings ever since I could remember, for I recognised my sensations for what they were, something quite different from the emotion of love. Kissing a young man I was fond of was a pleasure of the senses, whereas being in the same room as the person I was in love with was a joy of the whole being. To kiss the man one loved must be an ecstasy I could not even imagine.

The facts of life, as revealed to me by Mother at an age

when I had no interest in the subject whatsoever, had as much relation to the subtleties of sex as a diagram of the bile duct to the art of cooking and the refinements of eating, and therefore when one night a sudden glory of sensation burst upon me unsolicited, lighting up my whole mind and body with wondrous flame which somehow reminded me of the most beautiful of autumns, I believed that something unique had happened to me. I did not mention my experience to anyone, not because I felt the slightest sense of guilt or shame (why should I at such a marvellous happening?) but because it was something so glorious that I wanted in my selfish secret-iveness to keep it to myself. Besides, how could I have explained it? No one would understand because it could never have happened to anyone else. I believed it to be a new magic realm I had been allowed to enter, in compensation for banishment from the kingdom of imagination.

CHAPTER THIRTEEN

When Krishna and Nitya got back to England in June of the next year, 1923, they went to stay with Miss Dodge at Wimbledon, where they had often stayed before. Miss Dodge shared a house on West Side Common with her great friend, Muriel, Lady De La Warr, who was also a Theosophist. It was an intense excitement to be asked to West Side House when the boys were there, but these invitations were rare and never for more than the afternoon.

Miss Dodge was crippled with arthritis, and the whole time I knew her she was in a wheeled chair. She had an unusually deep, harsh voice and I stood in great awe of her. As for Lady De La Warr, who was small, waspish and sarcastic, I was not only very frightened of her but I disliked her intensely as well. The joy of being in Nitya's company, however, far outweighed any aversion I felt for my hostesses, and if it was fine and we could stay out in the garden, there was always the hope of avoiding them altogether. It was a big garden with a tennis court and shrubbery. (I found I could be truthful as well as impressive by telling people that I played tennis at Wimbledon.) The house was large, low and luxuriously furnished, and I remember very well Krishna's and Nitya's bedrooms which opened into each other, and their fitted wardrobes containing their neat suits and rows of brown shoes polished like horse-chestnuts, and stacks of fine shirts and handkerchiefs. Their clothes had almost as much charm for me as themselves.

I never went to West Side House by myself, but sometimes Betty and I would go there alone together by tube. We went down a few times to see the boys after they returned to England, and I noticed a new reverence towards Krishna in the people around him. But to me he seemed just the same, though more beautiful than ever. His was the eastern beauty of the Buddha with nothing effeminate about it. He was of about average height but looked shorter because he was so slim. Nitya was a couple of inches shorter and equally slender. I was more conscious than ever of the emanation of enchantment surrounding these two young men, and it was particularly strong at West Side House. I believe that court officials and members of a royal household experience much the same sort of glamour in palace life, from which they find it very hard to tear themselves away. Krishna and Nitya might well have been princes, with their air of aristocracy, their delicious fragrance, the best of everything surrounding them, their closely guarded privacy and the sense of privilege one had at being with them at all, let alone on terms of joking intimacy. I was acutely aware that there was hardly a Theosophist in the world who would not envy us knowing them as well as we did and seeing so much of them, and yet I did not know them nearly as well or see nearly as much of them as I should have liked. If only our own house had been big enough to accommodate them, for I never doubted that they would prefer to stay with us.

But apart from the general atmosphere of glamour, there was Nitya's special attraction for me, and I found myself more deeply in love with him every time I saw him. Now there was a new pain in it, though, a sense of thraldom which I had not known before. Unable to escape any longer into pretence, I was quite defenceless against the power of my feeling for him. When I parted from him now I could no longer throw off my depression after a few intense moments: it persisted for hours. I had been told that he was sad at parting from Rosalind and I resented her, but more as an unknown foreign influence drawing him away from England than as a personal danger, for in spite of my continued observance of magic rituals (the Ranelagh ticket had been kissed every single night since he had been away, and the mark on the wall every night we had been in London) I had no real hope of ever winning him for myself.

Instead of merely longing to see him, I now tried to worm out of Mother – without giving away my secret – when we were likely to meet again. I let her think it was Krishna I wanted to see, which seemed only natural to her, since she herself was never completely happy away from him. I found that now she knew I was interested she took me with her more often when she was going to see him, and as seeing him invariably meant seeing Nitya too, I cunningly encouraged her in her misapprehension.

I was naturally overjoyed when I heard we were to spend the summer holidays with them both. We were to go first to Vienna for a Theosophical Congress and then on to a place called Ehrwald, in the Tyrol near Innsbruck, which had been recommended for Nitya's health and where Krishna had been lent a house.

We started off on July 20, our party consisting of Krishna, Nitya, Marcelle de Manziarly, Rajagopal (the young man who had been with us at Boissy), an Indian couple called Patwardhan, an elderly Austrian, John Cordes by name, Mother, Betty and me, and two other girls whom we were to get to know very well. One of these was Ruth, an English girl of nineteen. Krishna had met her when he was in Sydney, where she had been staying for a while as a pupil of Mr Leadbeater. She was as dark as a Red Indian and had a lovely face, but she was too tall for complete beauty. The other girl, Helen, was an American of about the same age, whom Krishna had met just before he went to India in 1921, at a Theosophical Convention in Amsterdam where she was staying with her Dutch aunt. We were told that she was a reincarnation of Madame Blavatsky, the Founder of the Theosophical Society. She was not a pretty girl but she had abounding charm, and it soon became disagreeably apparent to us all that she was the favourite *gopi*. (We teasingly called Krishna's female devotees *gopis* after the name given to the milkmaids who played with Shri Krishna in Hindu mythology.)

I have since learnt that Mother knew all about Krishna's feelings for Helen because he had written to her before leaving for India to tell her that he had fallen in love and how miserable he was to be going away, but to me his devotion to Helen came as something hurtingly new. I had always felt that if anyone was his favourite it was I, though in truth I think he had managed hitherto to give each of his *gopis* the impression of being the favourite, just as Shri Krishna had

85

multiplied himself to the milkmaids so that each believed she was dancing with him. But now there was no mistaking his preference for Helen, and just because I felt I had lost Krishna, I began really to value him for the first time and became pettily jealous of Helen as well as disgusted with myself, for, not realising that my new emotion was one of the commonest in the world, I believed myself to be uniquely debased.

But some of the other *gopis* must have suffered far more than I. One of them in particular I knew to be dreadfully unhappy, and I knew too that Nitya with a wonderful sympathy was doing his best to help her. Perhaps for the only time in my life I saw Nitya objectively during those few days when he stood out from the fog of my love, and I came to realise what an extraordinarily sweet and understanding person he was and how much I loved him quite apart from being in love with him.

I have no recollection of Vienna beyond the boredom of the Theosophical lectures we were expected to attend and the frustration of seeing so little of the boys. We were staying at different hotels and did not always see them in the evenings. I remember, though, that the words *Bad Kammer* were written on the bath-mat in our hotel bathroom, so that every time I had a bath I felt I was piling up bad *karma* for myself and this added considerably to my depression.

When we got to Ehrwald, a small village in the mountains where we arrived on my fifteenth birthday, my old feeling for Nitya returned, intensified by my greater knowledge of him and remorse for my fickleness, and I soon fully recovered from my pique over Krishna's disaffection. I was comparatively happy during the eight weeks we spent there, although there was none of the intoxication of Boissy; but nor was there the philandering of Hemel Hempstead, for I could not feel any interest in anyone else while Nitya was there, and I had not yet learnt that most deadly of all feminine wiles, to flirt with one man so as to attract another.

I no longer had any personal jealousy of Helen, but I found her very irritating all the time we were at Ehrwald, because she employed innumerable little tricks to attract Krishna's attention (like myself with Miss Kershaw, only she was far more successful!), such as lagging behind with a stone in her shoe during a walk and expecting him to stop and take it out for her; and I suffered for the other *gopis*, including Mother, who I felt must be frantically jealous of her. But here I probably did them an injustice. Unlike myself they already regarded themselves as Krishna's disciples, and were striving to sublimate their personal feelings, and no doubt they looked upon Helen as a challenge If they could sublimate their feelings about *her* they must indeed be far along the road to perfection.

Even at Ehrwald I did not stay under the same roof as Nitya, but at least there was the soothing certainty of seeing him in a daily routine. He and Krishna, with Mother, Helen, Rajagopal and Cordes, stayed at the Villa Sonnblick, where we all had our meals, while the rest of us slept in another chalet about half an hour's walk away through the fields. Ehrwald was an isolated place, and our chalets were remote even from the village. We bought Tyrolean costumes and went for long walking expeditions. There was always some inn at the end of a walk where we could get a delicious vegetarian lunch and glasses of ice-cold buttermilk and a hip-bath (Cordes's panacea for all physical ills) in an icy mountain stream before setting off home. One day a travelling barber with a small guitar over his shoulder came to the inn where we were having lunch. He was a character straight out of *Lavengro* and I felt a stirring of longing for my Stretton days. What could growing up give me to compensate for my lost paradise?

After we had been at Ehrwald for about three weeks we began to learn a sonnet by heart each day, as it was thought to be a good way of increasing Krishna's vocabulary; and here I excelled. Being the youngest, my memory was the best, and besides I had always been able to learn by heart with ease. Nitya too had a gift for learning by heart, so an exciting rivalry grew up between us. I usually succeeded in beating him and he began to take notice of me. We sat next to each other at meals and he would often hold my hand under the table. He sometimes put his arm round my shoulders, though in quite a casual way, and once, when I had a headache, he made me lie down on his own bed (what rapture!) with a cold compress, and kept popping in to see how I was. He asked me one day what I intended to do in the future. I said that I knew myself but would not tell him (which was quite untrue, for I had not the slightest idea). The next day he asked me again and I answered that it would be of no interest to him, to which he replied, 'It is one of the few things that do interest me at present.' I had never been so pleased or flattered in my life.

Although I adored his attentions I did not take them as proofs of love, for I knew that both he and Krishna were wonderfully affectionate by nature. If anything, I felt left out of a secret circle while we were there. We had supper early and then those of us who were not staying at the Villa Sonnblick would be sent off to our own chalet. I suspected that for the others the important part of the day began only after we had been banished, though I did not know exactly what took place: I knew, however, that Krishna suffered some terrible, indescribable pain in his head and neck which lasted for an hour or more and of which one could see the ravages the next morning in his tired eyes. I also knew (Mother must have told me) that during that period of intense pain, the adult Krishna went away from his body, leaving the child Krishna behind – a small boy groaning in pain, and calling out for his Amma (his dead mother) and recalling small incidents from his childhood which he did not remember in his natural state. During these times when Krishna had 'gone off', the child could not for a moment be left alone.

Although I had been nurtured on the tenets of Theosophy I understood very little as yet of its esoteric side. I had heard of the Masters, of course, those supermen who, instead of being released from the wheel of life and death after they become perfect, elect to stay on this earth in order to help humanity in its struggle towards perfection; and I knew that they lived in Tibet and had physical bodies of great age, and that the mightiest of them was the Lord Maitreya who had taken the body of Jesus two thousand years ago, his own body being too sensitive for the everyday world, and that it was this mighty Being who was to take Krishna's body when the time came (the time was not far off, and the preparing of Krishna's body for this stupendous event was now becoming intensive);

88

but I had not yet *felt* the truth of any of this. It was an intellectual conception merely, though a very reasonable one.

I suspected that after we were banished from the villa each evening, one or other of the Masters, and perhaps even the great Lord Maitreya himself, appeared (in astral form, of course) and helped to prepare Krishna in some way for his great future. The astral body was that part of oneself which could move about at will on the astral plane, usually functioning only at night, when, during sleep, one could safely leave one's physical body; but there were certain psychic people who could leave their physical bodies at any time and rove round the world in the astral and move from place to place at the speed of thought, *and* remember their experiences on that other plane when they returned to the physical. I had been familiar with the astral ever since I could remember, and even now I cannot get away from the belief that I can go where I will in sleep (it is almost impossible wholly to discard the myths of one's earliest conditioning) but I have never remembered anything that happened on that other plane. Krishna, however, was psychic enough to be able to 'bring through' from the astral, and was constantly receiving messages and instructions from the Masters in this way which he would relay to Nitya, who was not gifted with second sight, to write down. (It was on the instructions of one of the Masters, for instance, that we started to learn a poem each day, but I did not find this out until much later.)

I knew, or guessed, enough of what was going on to realise that those who were allowed to stay at the villa while Krishna's preparation was going on were greatly favoured and I felt hurt and shut out at not being one of them. I have no doubt that Betty felt the same, but there was little communication between us in those days. We were developing along very different lines. Betty made great friends with Ruth and therefore had a companion during the evenings of solitude, whereas I had never had much gift for friendship, and, except when I was in love, preferred to be alone. Betty and I were to go through a great deal together in the next two years, but though we went through it side by side we were detached and quite incapable of helping each other. I was physically more mature than she, but she was already absorbed in an art. Moreover, she had a deeper spiritual sense and more feeling for nature and literature. We had even ceased to quarrel, which was the measure of the distance between us.

Krishna's preparation, whatever it was, stopped a few days before we left Ehrwald towards the end of September, and we were allowed to stay later at the villa. There were two tables in the dining-room, one large and one for two, by the window, where Mar de Manziarly and one of the others usually sat. Mar had to leave Ehrwald a few days before us, and on her last evening she asked Nitya to sit with her at the small table. In the middle of dinner he caught my eye, smiled, looked self-reproachful and kissed his hand to me. After this incident I wrote in a little notebook in which I made occasional entries that summer: 'N is perfectly delicious. I feel for him an unquenchable adoration, a mixture of filial, parental and fraternal devotion.'

On our last evening Nitya contrived that he and I should sit together at the small table by the window. As I sat down opposite him with shy joy, he said, 'I'll pretend I'm having a tête-à-tête in Versailles with the woman of my heart.' (Thereafter I looked upon Versailles as the most romantic place on earth and was dreadfully disappointed in it when I went there some years later for the first time.) Mar de Manziarly or Helen would have had the wit to play up to him, but I can be sure that I sat there dumb with shyness, and that was why Nitya said to me at the station the next morning: 'You are harder and more bottled-up than anyone I have ever come across.' Bottled-up maybe, but *hard*! According to Browning, Andrea del Sarto had said, 'What at bottom of my heart I wish for, if I ever wish so deep.' Those lines had struck me when I read them at school as being particularly applicable to myself in reverse. My real life was lived so deep down that I despaired of ever bringing it to the surface. Nitya's remark made me very unhappy, for it brought home to me my utter inability to reveal my true self to anyone, least of all to him.

Fortunately we were not to go straight home. Most of our party went on to Holland to stay a few days at Castle Eerde, near Arnhem. On the way we spent a night in Munich and I was temporarily shocked out of myself by the misery of the

German people. I was soon to see appalling poverty and disease in India, but nothing so startling and terrible as the look of hopelessness on the faces of the German women on the station platform at Munich.

Castle Eerde, an eighteenth-century moated castle of fawn brick, surrounded by several hundred acres of pine-forest, had been made over to the Order of the Star by Baron van Pallandt, but the transfer had not yet been completed and Philip van Pallandt was our host. Betty and I disgraced ourselves the first day by taking out a punt on the moat without permission, and Krishna (through Mother) was very angry with us (he was for ever blaming her for our bad manners and bad deportment), but on the whole those few days were intensely happy ones for me. It was the first time I had ever stayed in the same house as Nitya. On the first evening after dinner we sat on the floor round the log fire in the library with the lights turned low, and Nitya sat beside me and held my hand. Every evening after that, for as long as we were there, he held my hand sitting beside me in the firelight. Was his object to unbottle me, or was it just pleasant to have a hand to hold? Or was it that I was so silent and gauche that he looked upon me as more of a child than I really was? Of one thing I am certain, that he had no idea of the danger of the fire he was stoking. I never thought for a moment that he loved me, but for the time being I wanted no greater happiness than this, especially as I was not called upon to take any part in the conversation, which, as far as I can remember, was all about politics.

On each of those evenings, I wore a black satin dress inherited from Ursula, with an Irish lace collar, and this dress became so sacred to me that I refused to wear it again when I got home, or to part with it, to Nanny's understandable exasperation.

How I dreaded going back. London would mean all the restless misery of not knowing when I was going to see him, and soon he and Krishna would be going off to Ojai, and Ojai meant Rosalind. As I sat in the firelight with my hand in his, dreadfully cramped sometimes because I did not dare change my position by so much as an inch for fear he would draw away from me, I thought how wonderful it would be if a spell

91

could be put on us and we could remain like this for a hundred years – or, better still, for ever – and I tried to work such a spell by *willing* it to happen. I believed I should never be as happy as this again.

CHAPTER FOURTEEN

I started school as soon as we got home. Krishna and Nitya spent a fortnight at Wimbledon before returning to Ojai – a period of acute misery for me. What made it so painful was that we had no regular times for seeing them. We could not go to Wimbledon when we liked, nor could they ask us there, because they were very much guests themselves. We had to wait for an invitation from Lady De La Warr, and yet it never occurred to me to make myself pleasant to her so that she might ask me more often. Helen and Ruth were both staying at West Side House and I envied them dreadfully.

I saw Nitya only three times in those two weeks. Twice we went to Wimbledon for the afternoon and once he came to Mansfield Street. But there was another occasion when I might have seen him but was left behind. I came home from school one afternoon to find that Mother and Betty had gone to Wimbledon for the *night*. If I had been home in time I should almost certainly have gone with them. To miss the chance of sleeping under the same roof as Nitya, perhaps of having breakfast with him next morning, was more than I could bear. I rushed upstairs to the bathroom and in the family medicine cupboard found a bottle with NOT TO BE TAKEN printed on the label. I took out the cork and without any hesitation drank as deeply as I could. But very little of the stuff went down; it turned out to be glycerine for the hands. I was sick. And then came a deluge of tears such as I had never known before and have never allowed myself since. I was protesting against my thraldom and my defencelessness. I felt so ill afterwards that it cured me for ever of thinking that a good cry would do me good in an emotional crisis.

Ursula found me at last in my distress, without knowing the cause of it (I believe I made up some story about an unkindness at school), and she did a very sweet thing. She took me out to dinner in a restaurant with her great friend of the moment, Patricia Ward (they had come out together the previous season), and Patricia's old nanny. I had never before been to a restaurant in the evening (and only very occasionally for lunch, when Father took us to the Berkeley Grill for Mother's birthday on Boxing Day), and sure enough the 'change of scene' soothed me into temporary forgetfulness as it is reputed to do; but I was dreadfully shaken by my experience, and frightened to realise the power Nitya now had over me. I vowed that next time I would go to the laboratory at school and drink real poison.

The next day Betty told me that Nitya had asked after me. He had wanted to know what I would be doing when I got home from school and Betty had said, 'Prep probably.' He had then asked her what I was like with 'Society people', to which she had replied that I always adapted myself to my surroundings. (My comment on this in my notebook was, 'The traitor', although I was secretly pleased.) It was some comfort to hear that he had wanted to know about me, but I could not easily cast off the deep depression which followed my suicidal outburst.

For the first time I was unhappy at Queen's, and therefore when Mother suggested that I should accompany her to India, where she was again going with Father at the end of November, I jumped at the chance of such a complete change. I knew why Mother herself wanted to go to India: if she could not be with Krishna she would feel nearer to him in his own country, and besides, Uncle Victor had recently become Governor of Bengal and this in itself was a good reason for going – but why did she offer to take me? I am sure she did not know how depressed I was, for I always managed to hide my feelings, at any rate from her, but no doubt she thought I would be lonely that winter in London with Barbie and Robert both married, Betty 'finishing' in Paris, and Ursula going out to stay with the Lyttons in Calcutta.

I was sick in the train the whole way from Calais to Marseilles. Mother and I were sharing a sleeper and I was overcome, not only with physical misery but with shame at

94

being sick in front of her, for this was the first time I had ever been alone with her for long. To my great surprise, however, not only did she not appear to be in the least disgusted with me, but was every bit as sweet and comforting as Nanny would have been, holding my head and sponging my face. I realised for the first time that mothers were capable of ministering to their children. I was fifteen and had never come in contact with a child looked after by its mother.

I began to keep a diary after we got to Bombay on December 15, so from this time my story is well charted and does not have to depend on mere recollection. It was not a diary with dates but a thick exercise book with a soft black-leather cover.

Mother and I stayed with Ratansi in Bombay in his lovely house on Malabar Hill, looking over the harbour, while Father went straight off to Delhi. I was intoxicated with India from the moment we sighted land and the smell of spices came to us distinctly across the intervening water. I love to go back in imagination to Ratansi's long cool verandah with its green Tatti blinds, and hear again the flat tread of bare feet over polished wooden floors and the loud caw-caw of the crows flying against the sky at sunset. The warmth of Bombay was so delicious at that time of year – never oppressive but sufficient to give one 'a little gentle action of the skin' as Granny would put it. And then how beatific it was to be certain of waking day after day to a blue sky.

Ratansi's cleanliness fascinated me. He had a shower and changed his clothes at least four times a day, even though it was not really hot. I became very much aware while we were there of the inadequacy of our own habits – wearing our underclothes for a week, a dress until it got dirty (I had only brought four dresses with me); not rinsing ourselves after a bath but drying off the dirt on a used towel, and shaking hands with the right hand which had been used for the most intimate purposes. Ratansi kept a finger-bowl on his office-desk so that he could rinse his hand after being obliged to shake hands with a European. It was interesting to see ourselves through Indian eyes and not at all gratifying. I began to think for the first time that perhaps my own background was not the most perfect in the world.

Most of the Indian men we met in Bombay wore the little round white cotton cap of the Gandhi follower, and I, like Mother, soon became an enthusiastic adherent of Swaraj. We were provided with spools of cotton and went about spinning with thumb and forefinger – and spinning all the more diligently if we were in some place where we might be seen by the British.

After ten days in Bombay we set off with Ratansi and some other Indian friends for Benares to attend a Theosophical Convention. We were two nights on the train and I was much shocked and rather shy at having to share our compartment with Ratansi and another Indian man, but I soon became accustomed to travelling with men in our sleeper, and, as Mother pointed out, it was better than having to share it with strangers. The first-class compartments were for four. No bedding was provided and there was no corridor, but each compartment had its adjoining lavatory and wash-basin. Our bearer, Swami, whom we had chosen out of a crowd of servants waiting for employment on the docks at Bombay, made up our bunks into beds from our bedding-rolls and cooked our meals on a spirit-lamp in the lavatory.

At Benares I met Mrs Besant for the first time. She was treated like a queen by her followers, and naturally I was very awed by her at first, but she put me at my ease in an astonishing way. I had never seen anybody with such kind eyes looking at one with so much love that it was impossible not to feel secure and happy in her presence. Her mode of greeting was half-way between the English handshake and the Indian *namaskar*. She held out both her hands in the *namaskar* position on meeting me and pressed mine between them, and did this again on saying goodbye. I was surprised to find that she was so short, but she was sturdily built and must have been fat in her youth, because now, at seventy-six, her chins hung down in several layers of loose skin. Her hair was short, white and curly, and she always wore a white sari – white cotton for everyday and white silk for special occasions.

Mother and I stayed with Ratansi at the Maharaja's guest house overlooking the Ganges, but we went to have tea with Mrs Besant every afternoon at her house in the Theosophical compound. I realised that we were very privileged to see so

96

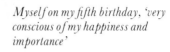

Myself on my fifth birthday, 'very conscious of my happiness and importance'

1908. Back row: Robert, Mother with Mary on lap, Barbie.
Front row: Ursula, Betty

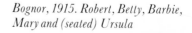

Bognor, 1915. Robert, Betty, Barbie, Mary and (seated) Ursula

My mother, Emily Lutyens, in 1912

My father, Edwin Lutyens

Krishna, London 1911

Nitya, 1920

*Venice, 1924. Krishna,
Rama Rao, Mother,
Nitya, Helen, Mary*

*Arrival at Bombay, 1924.
Nitya and Krishna with
Mrs Besant*

Barbie's wedding, May 10 1920, at the Savoy Chapel.
Hermione Lytton, Ursula, Kathleen Balfour, Mary,
Davina Lytton, Betty. We were dressed in cream lace with
gold sashes and wreaths and bouquets of forget-me-nots

Castle Eerde, 1923.
Helen, Mary, Betty, Mother (all in car),
Nitya, Krishna

Nitya in India, 1924

Leadbeater at the Manor, 1925

Myself aged eighteen in Holland, 1926

much of her, but I do not think it was merely the reverence with which she was regarded by those around her that produced in me a feeling of hero-worship. She seemed to me immeasurably greater than anyone I had ever met, and I am sure my nature was deeply enriched by knowing her. I had never felt like this about anyone before, nor have I felt it in the same degree about anyone since. She was rather shocked that I had been taken away from school, for she was a great upholder of higher education for women, and made out a list of books for me to read, which we afterwards ordered in Madras.

Pilgrims of all sects come to Benares to cleanse themselves in the holy river, and the sight of its banks in the early morning is as fascinating as any in the world. We took a boat at sunrise and were rowed slowly along close to the shore. The banks were swarming with men, women and children, performing their ablutions and holy rites, and washing their clothes. Whereas the men stripped to a loin cloth (except the *sanyasis* in their saffron robes), the women kept on all their clothes while bathing, so that their saris contrasted brilliantly with the steep stone steps leading down to the mud-coloured water. A little further along, at the burning ghats, smoke from the pyres rose up straight into the gentle morning sky. Something bumped against the boat, and looking over the side I saw to my horror that it was the dead body of a baby. Fuel was very expensive, so dead babies were often thrown into the sacred river along with bits of bodies that had not been consumed by the inadequate wood of the funeral pyres. There must be some extraordinary property in the water of the Ganges to immunise it against all the filth that goes into it. The rites of the pilgrims invariably include drinking the water as well as bathing in it, and, of course, spitting into it.

After ten days in Benares we went off to Allahabad where we stayed a couple of nights with Sir Tej Bahadur Sapru, the statesman and lawyer. Sapru's daughter, who was just my own age, was betrothed to a man she had never seen and was in a state of bubbling excitement, getting together her trousseau of beautiful saris. She was westernised to the extent that she had not been married at five years old. She showed me a miniature of her fiancé, a good-looking young man in a turban. She wore it in a locket round her neck. I was dreadfully envious of her and did not see that our western freedom had anything to offer compared to the easy settlement of one's future with a partner carefully selected by one's parents — always provided, of course, that the partner was young and handsome *and* an Indian. I too yearned for someone of my very own whose miniature I could wear round my neck.

I had written at the beginning of my diary (and on the fly-leaf of the subsequent volumes) Browning's poem:

> Round the cape of a sudden came the sea,
> And the sun looked over the mountain's rim —
> And straight was a path of gold for him,
> And the need of a world of men for me,

and it seemed to me that Sapru's daughter had her path of gold like the sun, whereas I had to return to the world of men. The world of men was everything I most hated — Society, conversation and dependence on others. I did not look upon having someone of my very own as a form of dependence: on the contrary that would be the perfect freedom. I had come to realise that I could not live alone, but with one other person (could it, could it ever be Nitya?) I would be independent of the whole world of men. When once I married, or had found *the* one person, I would never have to see anyone or talk to anyone else again.

In my envy, I told Sapru's daughter that all I cared about in the world was chemistry and mathematics, and that in a year or so I would be going to Cambridge where I would take higher mathematics. I hoped to strike a spark of envy in her, but merely succeeded, I believe, in arousing her pity.

CHAPTER FIFTEEN

We went next with Mrs Besant to Adyar, a few miles from Madras, the international headquarters of the Theosophical Society. It was the most beautiful place I had ever seen or could have imagined, situated where the Adyar river meets the sea. Most of the buildings that comprised the headquarters were by the side of the river, and a walk through a palm-grove led down to the coast with its miles and miles of empty white sands. We were greatly favoured in being allowed to stay in Krishna's and Nitya's own room with the best view in the compound, at the top of the building at headquarters where Mrs Besant lived, and we were looked after by their own charming servant.

We did not see much of Mrs Besant while we were there, because she went every day into Madras to the offices of *New India*, the daily newspaper she edited, but we made innumerable acquaintances among the Theosophists of all nationalities who lived in bungalows or blocks of flats scattered over the compound. We led an Indian life, keeping Indian hours, sitting on the floor for our meals and taking off our shoes before entering a room. We had coffee and toast at six in the morning, and the main meal of the day, called breakfast, at eleven; then tea at three and supper at half-past six. We had breakfast and supper in a communal kitchen. There were several such in the compound, and about a dozen people shared the one we used. Although it was called a kitchen it was in reality a completely bare, whitewashed room with a tiled floor leading off the real kitchen where the food was prepared. We sat cross-legged on the floor with banana-leaves in front of us to serve as plates. The bare-footed cook came in with brass vessels and ladled the delicious Indian food into little heaps on each leaf. Fortunately, Mother and I were provided with teaspoons, but all the others ate with their fingers, never using more than their finger-tips.

We slept on our verandah under mosquito-nets on *charpoys* – low beds made of plaited webbing with a thin quilted cotton mattress spread on top. There was the minimum of furniture in our room – a *chowki* (a large divan), a chest of drawers, a couple of chairs and some pegs on the wall. (The kingfishers skimming the river outside more than made up for the stark white walls.) In the adjoining wash-room there was a thunder-box and, for a shower, a duckboard over a hole in the floor on which one stood and poured water over oneself from brass pots brought in by the servants. The extreme simplicity of Indian life seemed to me to achieve a very high standard of civilisation, for there was nothing to distract one from the things of the mind and spirit. The uniform simplicity of the women's clothes attracted me greatly. How refreshing it must be never to have to think of fashion; to be able to keep one's clothes folded in a chest, and to pass them down from generation to generation.

Most of the European women who lived at Adyar wore saris like Mrs Besant, and I could see that Mother was longing to wear one too, but I managed to restrain her. Though it was the most beautiful and graceful of garments when worn by an Indian, the Europeans wearing it all looked ridiculous in varying degrees. It was something to do with their walk. They lacked the Indian grace which came from walking barefoot. I made friends with two delightful Indian sisters who showed me how to put on a sari, but I never wore one in public. These sisters surprised me by their extreme modesty. They would not even undress in the same room together, and when we went down to bathe they would not discard their towels until they were actually in the water, although there were no men present. And I had thought that I was unusually modest.

Mother received a letter from Krishna from Ojai welcoming us to his room. He told her that Rosalind was with them again that winter, taking care of Nitya, news which cast me down dreadfully.

I was at rather a loose end during the long siesta when the whole world seemed to go to sleep from mid-day until teatime. Like most young people I disliked sleeping in the

100

afternoon, so I managed to get through a good deal of reading. I tried unsuccessfully to read *Nicholas Nickleby*, the first Dickens I ever attempted on my own, and found how much he had gained from Mother's skipping. I had loved him when she had read him aloud to us, but I have never been able to finish one of his books myself. I then switched to *Crime and Punishment*, my first Dostoevsky, and was immediately enthralled. Perhaps Dickens did not have a fair chance in the glory of a south Indian winter, but I have read Dostoevsky in all manner of places, under the most varied conditions, and never has he failed to impose his own climate.

We made a day-trip to Conjeeveram from Adyar, to see the temples, and were entertained there by an Indian family who took their brass pots out into the fields when nature called them, but for Mother and me had provided what they considered to be adequate European accommodation – a chamber-pot on the roof without any screening whatsoever, in full view of all the neighbouring houses. I was fortunate in being able to wait until we got back to the comparative luxury of our private thunder-box, but for poor Mother who could not wait there was no alternative.

One other incident of importance to me occurred while we were at Adyar. We were invited to lunch by the Willingdons at Government House in Madras, and as soon as we arrived, an aide-de-camp rushed up to Lady Willingdon and I overheard him whisper to her in horror, 'It's only a little girl with plaits who's come.' My dignity was much affronted, for I felt myself to be completely grown-up, and to make matters worse I found that this same aide-de-camp was sitting next to me at lunch. I would love now to hear a recording of our conversation.

After four weeks at Adyar it was not easy to adapt myself to Government House, Calcutta, where we went next. Staying with the Lyttons we found Father, Ursula, Patsy Ward and Cecil Baring (afterwards Lord Revelstoke) with his two daughters, Daphne and Calypso, who were old friends of ours. I felt years older than Davina Lytton, my special friend and contemporary, who was leading a schoolroom life with a resident governess, and as all the other girls were 'out', I fell between two stools and was thoroughly miserable. I had been brought back wth a vengeance to the 'world of men'. I could not help resenting on behalf of my Indian friends the pomp and pretentiousness of Government House, and felt that I was in some way betraying them by staying there at all. It was not the fault of the Lyttons themselves (Mrs Besant thought very highly of Uncle Victor and of what he was trying to do for India, and therefore I exonerated him); it was the Anglo-Indian tradition which imposed its ridiculous customs and accoutrements – English hours, English food, stuffy English furniture, all so unsuitable to this climate – and the puffed-up self-importance of 'a little brief authority' on the native civilisation. And my poor Indians had to pay for all this ostentation which was put on to impress them. I was of an age when everything was clearly black or white, and in my eyes the British Raj was as unequivocally black as the villain of a Victorian melodrama.

My resentment was coupled with a sense of personal inadequacy. I wrote in my diary:

'Father isn't a bit pleased to see me, and I know he doesn't like me a scrap, which makes me rather miserable as I am very fond of him indeed. The whole atmosphere is unbearable. The house is upset at all four corners by quarrelling girls who scheme and spy. I miss Mummie dreadfully. True I see her every day – but we have been so much together and so near to each other for the past month or so. I think I love her more than anybody else in the world. She is wonderful, and beautiful inside. I am very proud of her and, I think, everyone adores her although they make fun of her. She certainly has the strength of her own opinions – which is a quality I admire immensely. I feel somehow that I shall never have such an opportunity again of being so near her – and that I have wasted it. She ought to be happy, as her presence has the power of making so many people happy – and it is lovely to be loved. I feel very depressed just now – and very friendless – but then I am of a morbid character. Ursie and I used to be such good friends once upon a time, but now we are oceans apart in everything. There is not one person in the world to whom I would tell my thoughts and feelings – not even

102

Mummie! – except myself of course. I often feel that I am the only person existing in my life and that all else is a creation of my fancy. But somehow I could not create such hypocrisy and reservation as I see all around me. Oh! for a friend to whom I could tell everything. Mummie was unhappy as a child – but she found a comfort in religion. I have no religion – no belief – no God – nothing! But I suppose life is worth living for the pure joy of being able to write. In Delhi I shall be happy, for I shall be free and not have to depend on other people's desires. Daphne, Calypso and Ursie can go their own way – flirt with their own chaps, dance at their own balls and burn their own boats.'

But I was not happy when we first got to Delhi, where the Barings and Patsy stayed with us. We travelled from Calcutta with Father, who would not take off his socks during the night journey in case there was an accident. He said he could not possibly walk along the cold railway lines in bare feet. We had our own house at Raisina (the first house Father built in New Delhi, then No. 1 Viceregal Estate, now No. 2 Willingdon Crescent), but though there was plumbing the water had not yet been laid on; it was bitterly cold (this was early in February) and the fire smoked. We were in the process of making a garden. The roses were wonderful – I have never seen such roses as in Delhi – but it always seemed to me that they were blue with cold.

Several young men came to stay and I felt more left out than ever. Mother spent a great part of the day in the Legislative Assembly, and as this bored me, and the others did not take me with them on their excursions, I was left very much on my own. I tried to go for walks by myself on the wasteland which then separated Raisina from Old Delhi, but on the second morning I was accosted by a man with a packet of indecent postcards which he tried to show me. I ran home as fast as I could and never dared venture out alone again. But during the latter part of our stay in Delhi, Wells's *Short History of the World* arrived, among other books ordered in Madras on Mrs Besant's recommendation, and once embarked on that I needed no other form of amusement. I learnt it almost by heart.

Soon after arriving in Delhi I heard that Mother was not coming back to England with us in March but was to wait until April so as to travel with Mrs Besant, who was going to London to give a course of lectures at Queen's Hall. 'That means coming back alone with Father and Ursula,' I confided in my diary, 'those two adoring each other. Father disliking me.' And yet I never did anything to make Father like me. It might have been so easy. He heard me singing one of Nanny's old songs one day – *Little Tottie Went to Ma* – and thereafter he tried to make me sing it on every occasion when we had visitors (and that was almost every day because an evening without guests was to Father a wasted evening); but I was shy and more often than not would flatly refuse, which must have seemed ungracious to him. How easy it would have been to sing it to please *him* whenever he asked for it, but, oh, how I wished that he would not ask. It was a long song with several verses and I was afraid of boring people with it. Ursula and Patsy used to sing to their ukuleles even before they were asked, and charmed everyone. They had one song in particular for which they had written the lyrics, beginning, 'I am weary of the ballroom, said the girl,' sung to the tune of 'I am weary of the garden, said the rose,' which was always an immense success.

But before we left for England I was to spend a heavenly few days away from the world of men. I went with Mother and some of our Indian friends to Mattra and Brindaban, Shri Krishna's birthplace. It was heaven to get back to what I thought of as *my* India and to be again in the company of Indians with whom I felt completely at my ease. The atmosphere of our bungalow in Delhi, like Government House in Calcutta, was not India at all but a horrible little piece of usurping England set down in this most fascinating and beautiful of countries, where Mother and I, we told ourselves, must often have been born in past incarnations.

One of the results of this trip to India was to give me for years a stupid hatred and contempt for everything British. It is only in middle age that I have had the joy of rediscovering the England I loved so much in my Stretton days.

CHAPTER SIXTEEN

When I got back to London the term was too far advanced to make it worth while returning to school, but I was to go back for a last term in the summer. What with the Easter holidays, there were now nearly eight weeks to be filled in without any organised work, and I set myself a programme of intensive reading of the books I thought I *ought* to read, including poetry. Page after page washed across my brain – I finished every book to schedule – and I do not remember a single line or idea out of any of them. If I found myself in any danger of becoming interested I hurried on for fear of not finishing the chapter by the stroke of the clock. And yet they were not wasted weeks, for on looking back and realising that I had absorbed *nothing*, I was shocked into vowing that I would never, never be so foolish again, and I never have – in that way.

The only outward change in my life was that I was now allowed to stay up to dinner in the dining-room, but I did not particularly enjoy my new status. There was no conversation when we were alone, because Father always brought his book or a chess problem into the dining-room (or the crossword as soon as crosswords came in) and Mother did the same when she was at home. We separated immediately after dinner. We never read aloud now or played card games or round games of any kind. As Nanny had taken to using our night-nursery as her sitting-room, and Betty was still in Paris, and Ursula usually out at a party, I had the day-nursery to myself, and there I would sit crouched over the perpetually smoking fire, reading with one eye on the clock. I did not speak more than a dozen words throughout the day.

When I returned to Queen's for my final term I found I had outgrown it. I felt infinitely older than any of my contemporaries; the college rules seemed ridiculously trivial and I was disgusted with the narrowness of the history that was taught to us. I was restless and dissatisfied. And then quite suddenly in the middle of the term faith burst upon me to intoxicate me with joy. It was as if the core of my being had cracked open and let in the light. I *knew* that God was everything and in everything; that there was *nothing* that was not God. Those lines from the *Bhagavagita* which Mother had so often quoted to me I now understood fully: 'I am the gambling of the cheat; the splendour of splendid things am I.' Life became all at once most beautifully simple.

Simplicity is the characteristic of all great joy and of all revelation. Requited love, the purest ecstasy that most of us know on earth, has pre-eminently this sense of simplicity, of everything being beautifully solved – at any rate in the early stages. Even if outside circumstances make its fulfilment impossible, at its first revelation everything falls into place within one with the smoothness of an intricate but exquisitely made piece of machinery.

Once under laughing gas I discovered the why and wherefore of existence, and woke, laughing and laughing, because it was all so absurdly simple. Why had I not thought of that before? Why had not anyone thought of it? I opened my mouth to tell the anaesthetist the ridiculous truth, but it had gone before I could get a word out. This experience has left me with an unpleasant suspicion that the solution really may be so ludicrously simple that when we do learn what it is all about (perhaps after death?) we shall *have* to laugh at its absurdity; that we humans have been given the gift of laughter so that one day we may appreciate the huge joke of creation.

I did not finish the term, although I forget how I got out of it, and on July 1, Betty (back from Paris), Ruth (who had been with us at Ehrwald) and her mother Mrs Roberts, Nanny and I went off for a fortnight to Church Stretton where we stayed in lodgings opposite the workhouse, about a mile from Carding Mill Valley. For the whole time we were there my exaltation remained to intoxicate me, and for the first time I began to look outside myself, to use my eyes, to see God in a rose and in a blade of grass and in the shadows chasing each other up the Caradoc.

Ruth and Mrs Roberts talked to us a great deal about the Masters and the Path of Discipleship and the need to prepare ourselves for the Coming of the Lord. How would we have felt, they asked us, if we had been living two thousand years ago in Palestine and had not been ready to receive the teaching of Jesus? The dry ethics of Theosophy blossomed in my mind and scented my heart. Ruth impressed upon us our tremendous good fortune, or, rather, our good *karma*, in being so close to Krishna – in having known him all our lives – and in now being given the fantastic opportunity of serving him. We could be Marys and Marthas to him. I began to feel that my name was perhaps symbolical.

How could we serve him? we asked. By making ourselves worthy, Ruth replied promptly; by getting into touch with the Masters, who were the great inner guides of Theosophy, and by taking as many steps as possible along the Path of Discipleship. First there was the step of Probation, when your chosen Master agreed to try you as his pupil; then Acceptance, when he linked his consciousness to yours, and then Initiation, when you joined the Great Brotherhood and could never again be deflected from the Path. There were five Initiations in all, and after passing the Fifth you were released from the wheel of life and death.

I was fascinated to learn from Ruth that Mrs Besant and Mr Leadbeater had already taken their Fourth Initiation; that Krishna had passed his Third and Nitya his First, and that Helen had been put on Probation at Ehrwald. It seemed to me that if Helen could take a step, so could I. She was not to my way of thinking at all a holy person. But Ruth was, and I was not surprised when she told us that she had been put on Probation in Sydney.

We were once more to spend the summer holidays with Krishna and Nitya, and Ruth tried to make us see that this was something quite different from just being with the people we were fond of in beautiful surroundings. It was the stupendous privilege of spending several weeks in the close proximity of the World Teacher-to-be. Had we ever considered why this privilege had been given to us – little insignificant us? Because the great Lord Maitreya himself thought us capable of becoming worthy to serve him when he

107

came. It did not matter what we *did*; it was what we *were* that mattered. We must *be* great; we must become great.

How could we become great? Ruth had no doubts. By eliminating self, by getting rid of all pettiness, jealousy, ambition and personal love. Yes, of course, that was the way. It was too easy for words. I would do it immediately.

Ruth suggested that fasting was a great help in getting rid of self, so I fasted for a whole day and found the time dragged almost unbearably without any digestive division between morning and afternoon.

I wrote to Mother and told her that I now felt ready to become one of Krishna's disciples and a pupil of the Master. This avowal did not come easily. Indeed I hesitated for days before summoning up courage to write, and I am sure I would have been too shy to tell her by word of mouth. Mother replied that I should write to Krishna himself, but this I simply could not do. Mother, therefore, promised to tell him for me and ask him if he would start teaching us when we were together in the summer.

In June Ursula had become engaged to Matt Ridley, and Mother had written from Northumberland, where she and Ursula were staying with Ursula's future sister-in-law. Mother told me that Ursula was going to be married in October, and I noted priggishly in my diary: 'Being in love has brought out all the best side of Ursie's character. I think it's an excellent thing – that is, if there is really no chance of her wanting or working for the greatest thing in the world. I wrote her a long letter full of sisterly affection.'

Poor Nanny felt very much neglected while we were at Stretton, for when we were not talking about the Masters and discipleship, which she thought quite mad, Mrs Roberts was reading Tolstoy's *Resurrection* to us. Nanny detested Theosophy, which had deflected so much of Mother's interest from the nursery. She was thankful that Barbie, Robert and Ursula had escaped its contamination and she was appalled that Betty and I were now becoming infected. I had a very sad scene with her in which she cried and declared that none of us wanted her any more; her mother had warned her against giving up her life to other people's children; the babies grew up and forgot you. She knew it could not be helped; it was inevitable that we should cease to want her, but sometimes we said things to wound which made it doubly hard. It was difficult to comfort her because I knew it was true that we had outgrown her. Her tragedy was that she had stayed with us too long, and yet at no time could we have borne to part with her. She was over fifty and was too much bound up with the family to uproot herself. I was the last of her babies, and even I had left school now. I dearly loved her still; I could never stop loving her, but I did not need her any more and it was vital to her to be needed.

She went through a bad time for some years after this, until she eventually found fulfilment again in looking after Barbie's children when their own nanny was on holiday. Wisely she would not take on another baby and have her heart broken all over again. She continued to live at Mansfield Street, growing younger-looking and smarter as she grew older, and we all borrowed her in turn when we needed a stopgap of any kind. I certainly borrowed her savings as well as her services when in need. She got me out of many a tight place in the early days of my marriage, and, knowing how hard-up I was, would bring me many little treats and save me many an expense by putting down small items for me to Mother's account.

In 1938 she died of cancer of the liver, having been in our family for forty years. Father designed her headstone with five angels on it to represent us five children. That was perhaps the most wonderful thing about her – however much we hurt her, we always remained her little angels. Father used to tell us that he was bound to go to heaven because his mother, who was a saint, would certainly be there and it could not be heaven for her without him. I think we can say the same about Nanny and ourselves.

CHAPTER SEVENTEEN

Krishna and Nitya arrived in England while we were still at Stretton. They had been in Ojai since the autumn. Helen, who had been back for a year to her home in New York, returned to England with them, while Rosalind went off to Sydney to be helped along the occult path by Mr Leadbeater. It was Krishna's wish that Mother, Betty and I should also go to Sydney to be trained by Mr Leadbeater, and as soon as Mother got my letter telling her that I was ready to become a disciple (I imagine she received a similar letter from Betty) she cabled to Leadbeater, whom she had met in her early Theosophical days, asking whether he would have us.

I knew that meeting Nitya again was going to be the first test of my new-found spirituality, and I half dreaded returning to London and half longed to meet the challenge.

I was not left long in doubt as to the strength of my new faith. Five minutes in Nitya's company and I was hopelessly bewitched and enslaved again. I rebelled against my thraldom but could not escape from it.

It was to Pergine that we went that summer, near Trento in the Dolomites, to an eleventh-century castle on the top of a steep hill which had been turned into a hotel. Our party was the same as the year before, except that Mar de Manziarly was not with us, but in addition there were two Indians, Jadu and Rama Rao, and a young Indian lady doctor, all of whom I had met in Adyar. We arrived on August 16 after sitting up all night in the train, a journey I never wanted to end because I sat next to Nitya and he encouraged me to sleep with my head on his shoulder.

Krishna, Nitya, Mother, Helen and Rajagopal occupied a square tower in the Castle grounds, while Betty, Ruth and I were in a round tower at the opposite corner. (Although

110

Helen was still privileged in being the only girl to stay under the same roof as Krishna, I got the impression that she was not quite such a favourite as she had been the year before, or perhaps Krishna had become more impersonal.) The rest of the party were dispersed in the main part of the Castle-hotel. Each tower had its own bathroom where the water was heated by a wood-burning stove which we had to stoke ourselves. The stacks of neatly-chopped wood were hiding-places for scorpions which terrified me.

We all had our meals together in the hotel dining-room, but were completely shut off from the other guests by high screens, and we had brought with us our own vegetarian cook, an Austrian provided by Cordes. From the Castle there were glorious views of snow-tipped mountains and of a blue lake, a few miles away, where we went to bathe during the first week of our stay.

For Krishna I felt a new reverence and shyness, which was partly due to Ruth's influence and partly to my own new receptiveness and understanding; but also, I think, because Krishna himself had grown in spiritual stature. His strange preparation began again a few days after we arrived, but it started earlier this summer and we were banished from the square tower at about five and did not see its occupants again until the next morning. We would all meet again in the square tower at eight o'clock for a quarter of an hour's meditation before breakfast, when Krishna would read us a passage out of *The Gospel of Buddha*, and then join with Nitya and Rama Rao in chanting a *mantram*. After breakfast we would go down to a large flat field, a short distance from the hotel through some vineyards, and play rounders or volley-ball. For the first few days, after playing games, we would lie on the grass while Mother read Indian history aloud, but gradually, urged on by Mother, Krishna began to talk to us of the purpose for which we were there. He was very shy at first and so were we, but this soon wore off and he talked more and more openly. Occasionally one of the others would join in, recounting some spiritual experience or difficulty overcome.

These talks, when Krishna would sit a little apart from us under some apple trees, with his knees hunched up to his chin and his fingers playing with the long damp grass at his feet, became the highspots of my day, although for those in the square tower the day did not really begin until we were banished. For me certainly the evenings from five o'clock were very long and lonely. We had no common sitting-room, and for some reason Betty, Ruth and I did not in the evenings mix with the other members of the party. We had an early dinner together and then immediately separated. I had a room to myself at the top of our tower where I read (it was mostly Turgenev and Meredith that summer) and wrote in my diary and tried to write stories, but for the most part I would sit at the open window looking down at the village of Pergine, watching the colour drain out of the sky and the lights go on in the village, wishing I was down there in the café from which, on very still evenings, I could hear faint music. We never once went down to the village during the whole of our six weeks' stay at the Castle.

Nitya also occasionally talked to us in the mornings. He believed he could help us, he said, because at one time he had 'been drawn away from all these things' but had found his way back again. He told us something about his and Krishna's early experiences at Adyar after Mr Leadbeater discovered them, and about the wonderful way in which Leadbeater had trained them.

Once when he was talking I tried the experiment of minutely and critically observing him in an effort to disenchant myself. What was it that was so lovable about him? Why could I not resist this attraction which was making me so unhappy? If I could understand the nature of it, perhaps I should be able to free myself. He was wearing grey flannel trousers and an open-necked shirt, which revealed his smooth brown throat, and he had Indian sandals on his bare feet.

The experiment was a complete failure. I succeeded merely in so imprinting his every feature on my mind that I continued to see his image after I shut my eyes. It had been like looking into the sun or into an electric-light bulb. There was not a hair on his head or a vein in his hand which did not enchant me.

The next day I wrote in my diary: 'I feel for him what should be the ideal feeling of a mother for a child. An absolute unbounded tenderness, a love or even adoration

112

which sweeps one off one's feet and leaves you breathless with rapture – wondering if there can possibly be another created thing so delicious as he; and an intense longing to render him service – and literally to lay down one's life to save him one spasm of pain. It is a feeling like this which one should have for the whole world – then indeed would one's task be easy.'

At the end of August Mother received a reply from Mr Leadbeater saying that he did not oppose the idea of our going to Sydney. After this encouragement Mother decided that we should go to India with Krishna and Nitya in November, and then all go on to Australia together in March. It never occurred to me to wonder what Father would say to this extravagant plan. Perhaps I felt that he did not care what happened to us, but more likely I took it for granted that Mother would get her own way, as she always seemed to do. Anyway, there was no doubt in our minds that we would go. I wanted to go very much. I was not being pushed in any way. Whatever I did or did not do in my adolescence, I always had at least the illusion of perfect free will.

I had heard a certain amount about Mr Leadbeater, particularly from Ruth who had a great reverence for him. I knew that he was an old man with a white beard because I had seen photographs of him, and I also knew that he had been a curate in the Church of England for some years, first in London, then in Hampshire, but had given up his parish when he met Madame Blavatsky. Nitya had told us how Leadbeater had gone with her to India, and how on the way she had set him some difficult tasks to do so as to test his obedience; one of these was to carry a full chamber-pot along the deck in broad daylight when all the passengers were sitting there. He claimed that she had completely changed his character in seven weeks.

I had also heard of his reputation for immorality with boys, but Mother declared this to be quite unfounded, and Krishna and Nitya were both staunch in maintaining that they had seen no vestige of immorality while he was training them. There had been a great scandal, however, in 1906, as a result of which he had been forced to resign from the Theosophical Society, but had been reinstated three years later by the almost unanimous vote of the General Secretaries throughout the world. This ordeal was said to be the symbolic crucifixion through which every candidate for the Arhat, or Fourth, Initiation must pass.

Nitya had also told us something about Leadbeater's early life. He had been born in Northumberland in 1847 but had spent most of his boyhood and early youth in South America where his father was a railway engineer. During these years he and his younger brother had been kidnapped by a band of half-caste rebels. The brother had been murdered for refusing to stamp on the cross, and Leadbeater himself tortured before he managed to make his escape. Later he had sought out the murderer, fought a duel with him and was just on the point of killing him when a vision of his dead brother appeared and begged him to spare the man's life, which he did. When the family returned to England, Leadbeater went to Oxford, but he had been there only a short time when the bank where the family fortune was deposited failed and he was forced to leave. After that he became a clerk in an office and later went into the Church. It was in 1884, when he was thirty-seven, that he met Madame Blavatsky, and he seems to have left his parish at Bramshott with no more than a few days' notice, to follow her to India. In Ceylon, on the way to Adyar, he became a Buddhist. He had not been many months at Adyar before he was urged by his occult master to awaken *kundalini*, the serpent fire of clairvoyance. This process was accomplished after forty days and nights of intensive and often agonising meditation, during which he was unable to eat or drink anything, but at the end of it he had developed the power of using astral sight while still retaining full consciousness in the physical body, and was also able to recall his past lives, the most remarkable of which had been in the fifth century B.C. in Greece, when he had studied at the school of Pythagoras.

Although I was anxious to meet Leadbeater, my real reason for going to Sydney was that it would keep me close to Nitya. For months ahead I could now see a future in which I would be with him, and nothing else mattered to me.

When once it was decided that we were to go, Krishna doubled his efforts to prepare us for such a great opportunity and to make the Masters more real to us. We *must* change

114

ourselves, that was the burden of his teaching. It was such *fun* to change. We must become great; we must do away with all pettiness; we must live dangerously. Above all we must not be bourgeois or mediocre. (He used these two words over and over again.) The three outstanding qualities to possess for discipleship were unselfishness, the power to love, and sympathy. And, of course, we must have complete mental and physical cleanliness. We must banish all sensual thoughts and live continually as if we were in the presence of the Masters. But we must not *suppress* feeling. Even the Masters could not approach us if we did that. Many Theosophists had made the mistake of killing their natural feelings because it was so much easier to kill than to transmute, but love was the basic law of existence and we must learn to love greatly. We must say to ourselves: 'I have every feeling in the world, but they are all subservient to my will.' Loneliness would become greater and greater as we advanced along the Path. It was human nature to wish for marriage and companionship and a home, but we could not have those things *and* serve the Master too. We must make the choice.

As well as the morning talks under the apple trees, Krishna now began to talk to us privately, each in turn, in the early part of the afternoon. My diary has preserved the atmosphere of those talks. 'Today I went over to rest at the Square Tower and there had an hour's talk with Krishna. He first of all began as he always does, "Well, Mary," repeated at intervals while I remain inarticulate and look stupid. He said that I must talk to him this time, which I proceeded to do in a very bad manner – trying to tell him how things stood with me – but not being able to do so – perhaps for the reason that I don't know myself. He wanted then to know why I wished to become a pupil of the Master – which I found difficult to answer. He wanted to make quite sure that it was not because everyone around me was trying to become one and I wanted to have a shot at it. I tried to convince him that this was not so – but that I had a feeling inside which was rather spasmodic.

'I must say he seemed to understand wonderfully. He said that one of the first things was to have an open mind – which I had not got – that it was almost disgraceful that I had so many prejudices and fixed opinions which formed terrible barriers.

He said that I had an over-developed mentality but that I had altogether left behind my emotional development. He then asked me a blank question: I desired something, knew what was in the way, was positive of my power to get over the obstacles – but why didn't I get there? A question which I have asked myself many times before. In the end he answered it himself – because I had not yet decided that it was worth while giving up my whole life.

'He said that I had never yet discovered anything strong enough to take me out of myself. He said that I must feel so acutely that I should be able to jump out of the window. He said I was too damned calculating and like an iceberg. How flattered I should have been a few years ago at this remark – how miserable it makes me now.

'He said many more things which I cannot remember in detail, but nothing can portray the enthusiasm which lit up his eyes. I could see the abnormal effort he was making to drum his eagerness into me. I know quite well, as he said, he would give his very life to help ("to make you happy for the rest of your life in whatever you do I would honestly – I'm not joking – give my life") and yet it was quite impossible for me to respond.'

And a few days later:

'This afternoon I had another talk with Krishna. He came in when I was lying on Mummie's bed reading Gilchrist's *Life of Blake* and we soon launched into a disjointed conversation. He was delighted to hear I felt beastly and took it as a good omen. He began by saying, "How's the iceberg getting on?" He pointed out all the disadvantages of being unfeeling – and all the selfishness of it. He said I must get rid of the layers of brick which I had plumped on the top of my natural instincts – that it was disgraceful to be so lethargic – especially at my age – that I had a heavy body which was in the way – that I gave myself away at every movement – when I played games, walked or talked. The reason for this state of affairs was quite evident. I had seen Betty getting into tempers, etc., and instinctively I had said, "Well, I shan't let myself be like that." And now he could see every day, I had a feeling of irritation, of affection which was gone in a minute. That this self-recollectedness could be of marvellous utility if used in the

116

right way, but as I used it, it was simply stunting the natural growth of something. He said that if once I made up my mind to change – and I must change at once – that I could beat them all – get along with great strides – that he felt this in his very bones. That I had some excellent things but needed those little weaknesses which balanced the scale – that I could beat them all because I had a touch of genius. He said: "Supposing someone comes to you and says that they are in love with you – ready to go to the other end of the earth for you – to worship you: what would you do? You'd take it quite calmly and say, "All right – go on then."

'He said that when he saw me it was like some beautiful rose that was being maltreated every day. That from morning till night he was thinking of me – of how he could help me – that even two years ago when he woke up to all this, he had thought then – will Mary come to it? He said that if only it was assured we could all be together working in the future he would be happy. That he had been fond of me ever since he first knew me as a baby. But I must – must – must change.

'He sat there drumming his enthusiasm into me – nothing could have equalled his sincerity. He was just wonderful (most inadequate praise). None of us realise how really great he is – working, working, working – and how I would have given my life to have helped him one little inch – instead of which I only caused him greater suffering by my unresponsiveness. I wanted to scream out – "By God, you wait. I'll show you that I can change" – but my tongue stuck in my throat (selfishness). But he was moved so greatly by his earnestness and desire to help me that he began to shed tears. I forgot myself then in my devotion to him – and I said what he wanted me to say. I won't wait any longer now till I get inspired. I'll work for his sake as Mummie has always worked. I won't add to his suffering. I will strive my utmost to relieve it.'

And after ten days in which I made no entry in my diary, except for some sketches for stories, I wrote:

'I have had more wonderful talks with Krishna – in one of which he made me weep – urging on me the need for immediate effort in case the vision of the mountain top should fade away. In the last talk it was I who nearly made him weep – and he finished by saying that no one would ever love me so much as he does – that none of us know what real love, real devotion is, that he wanted to see me great, happy and beautiful – and that if his had been an ordinary life he would have asked me to marry him long ago!'

CHAPTER EIGHTEEN

Krishna's pounding away at us; the long lonely introspective evenings; the need I felt to change myself radically and give myself to *something* with drastic abandon; all were leading up to a crisis. We had only three more weeks at Pergine and I must not leave it the same person as I had arrived. Something must happen; something must break. Whether what finally did happen was the result of sudden impulse or long deliberation I am not sure, but there came a fateful day, September 12, when I told Mother that I felt Nitya could help me more than anyone and that I should like to talk to him alone. She must have passed this on to him that very evening, for next morning he took my arm as we were walking down to the playing field and said how glad he was that I felt he could help me, and if I would come to the square tower that afternoon we could have a talk.

I went to Mother's room in the square tower after lunch, and in due course Nitya came to me there. Mother went into another room when he appeared, as she did when Krishna talked to me, and we were left alone.

It can perhaps be imagined what I felt on this occasion of my first real talk with him after all those years of loving him in secret. It might be the one and only chance I would ever have of talking to him, and I was determined not to waste it by shyness. Before the end of the interview, with the courage of jumping out of the window, I had completely given myself away to him. We talked for nearly an hour and a half. He said that he always thought of people as trees, and that I was like a sapling whose roots had been so starved that the leaves were nearly dead. He said to me: 'When you pass your first Initiation I shall be the happiest man in the world.' What then, I asked myself, was there left for me to do but pass it as soon as possible? I told him that I would always take his word for everything, that I would do anything in the world for him, and that ever since I could remember I had loved him more than anybody in the world.

Afterwards I wrote in my diary: 'There is a meaning now in everything – something which cries to me spontaneously in the birds, the insects, the trees. I have something in common with all – oh, don't you understand, my heart, what is peeping out from me? Oh, freedom, freedom, I feel you for the first time. Beauty is shining forth. There is the smell of orange blossom in the air – from the trees hang golden fruits – there is a real pearl on every blade of grass.' I felt cleansed in my ecstasy, having at last given away my secret. I compared myself to an empty gourd from which all the rottenness had been scooped out and which was now ready to be filled with the waters of life.

That first talk with Nitya lasted me for nearly a fortnight, but we were leaving on the 28th and I longed to talk to him again, to have some words of his to cling to during the weeks in London before we all set off for India.

On the morning of the 25th he and I walked down to the playing field together arm-in-arm and just as we got there I managed to ask him whether I could talk to him again before we left. He said, of course; we would talk that afternoon. He would come to me in our own round tower.

I described this second interview in my diary:

'Directly after lunch Nitya began talking to Ruth, so I did not get a chance of knowing where or when he was coming to me – but he sent a message by Rajagopal to say that he would come to our tower at a quarter past two. So I had 45 minutes of expectant waiting – trying to read but not understanding a word. He came and we lay on my bed and talked till 4 o'clock. [We lay on the bed because there was nowhere to sit in the room except for one very hard upright chair.] He talked of Probation and the reality of the Masters – then of me – and lastly I told him of the difficulties of self-expression – that I had so much I wanted to say to him but was unable to give vent to it. He has such a wonderful power of sympathy and I recognise the seed of true greatness in him. He is constantly saying to me: "You will be a wonderful person."

120

'We also talked a little of Amma [Mrs Besant. Amma, meaning mother, was the name by which many of her followers called her] and of the story of how she curtsied to one of the A.D.C.s in Calcutta thinking him to be Uncle Vic. Nitya said that such an incident would have made him boil with shame – or anyone if it had happened to them – but that Amma was so really "big" that she laughed delightedly at herself. Would any of us have done likewise? And we thrilled to think of her and hugged each other all the more.'

On the 27th I made my final Pergine entry:

'Tomorrow we shall be gone. Will we ever realise what this time has meant – will anything again be so wonderful? This morning the rain clouds cleared away and the sun shone forth and the air was blue and the breeze soft – all contributing to make happy the last day. At meditation Krishna read of the Lord Buddha's final entrance into Nirvana and of the venerable Ananda (his favourite disciple). I still feel too shy to show any mark of reverence to the pictures in the meditation room (these consist of one of the Lord Buddha and a number of smaller ones of the Masters) though my instinct is to go down on my knees to them. Walking down to the field I told Nitya my favourite limericks. We had three bad games on a piece of ground that was swilling in shiny brown mud – then at 11 o'clock we climbed up the hill to the apple trees and sat on a wet grassy bank. Krishna talked more wonderfully than ever – about real unselfishness and faith – saying that to be a disciple was the only, only thing that mattered. All the while I lay on the rug beside Nitya and I felt for the first time pure unselfish devotion. He was so tired and I ached all over to convey to him something soothing and helpful. But he gave me more than I could ever be able to give him – a real sense of bliss – he was so thoughtful and so loving and responsive – and I would have gone down on my knees to him but had to content myself with kissing his hand – which he returned.

'I feel the Masters growing more real every minute – nearer and more beautiful – and I have found them as the centre of my life for all eternity and not myself: I am a dot on the circumference now, and though to tread the radius which lies between us may take many, many, many lives – I know that I will not cease until I reach the centre. Two things have been

121

instrumental in making all this more real. One is that I have been reading the Gospel stories and have found in them a new meaning and have felt an intense, almost personal love for the Christ – and the second reason is the message that was read to us on the morning of the 25th. This – which I write below – was given to us through Krishna by the Lord Himself [the Lord Maitreya]. There was much more of it but K was too tired to be able to transmit it all.

'"Learn to serve me, for along that Path alone will you find Me. Forget yourself and then only am I to be found.

'"Do not look for the great Ones when They may be near you.

'"You are like the blind man who seeks sunshine and He is your sunshine.

'"You are like the hungry man who is offered food and will not eat. The happiness you seek is not far off. It lies in every common stone. I am there if you could only see. I am the Helper if you will let Me help."

'There is much to do when I get back to London. I have no doubt that after this it will seem very hard – the other life very meaningless – but if you are one pointed in the thought that discipleship is the only thing in the world "then everything becomes simple" as Krishna would say.

'Nitya said that he was very glad I was going back to London as it would show whether I was capable of still remaining open or whether the London atmosphere would immediately undo all that Pergine had done (you bet it won't!).'

122

CHAPTER NINETEEN

It was easy enough to dedicate my life to the service of the Masters with Nitya being loving and responsive on a rug beside me, but back in London the old misery began again of never knowing when I was going to see him. I had not been dishonest, though I may have been self-deceived, in maintaining that I wanted to become a disciple more than anything in the world: I had just not realised that happy love fills one with all those longings for self-sacrifice, dedication and service which are felt to be essentially religious. The 'sense of bliss' Nitya had given me was little different from spiritual ecstasy. It intoxicated me with the same exquisite feeling of cleanliness, unselfishness and simplicity, the one great difference being that it needed constant reassurance to feed on. We can imagine that God's love for us is unvarying and unending, but no amount of imagination could deceive me into thinking that Nitya was anything but fundamentally indifferent to me on the few occasions when I met him in London after our time at Pergine. Before that I had been able to bear his indifference (I had borne it for years while my love was a decent secret) but not now – not now that confession had somehow besmirched it.

We had a month in London before we set off for India. On October 13 Ursula was married at St Margaret's. I have far less recollection of her wedding than of Barbie's, four and a half years earlier, perhaps because I played no part in it (she had only small children as attendants), but most probably because I was immured in my own private hell. I remember very well, though, the two weeks we were in London before her wedding. (It seems incredible that Mother returned from Italy only a fortnight before having a daughter married with full panoply.) Ursula and her fiancé were so much in love that they held hands all through meals, and he sent her flowers every morning. Her happiness accentuated my own heartache. What affected me most, however, about her marriage was that Annie was going with her as her personal maid. I felt this parting acutely because I was very intimate with Annie (almost more so even than with Nanny) and had always looked upon her as belonging especially to me. If I had not been going away myself, her loss would have been even greater.

Mother did not find it easy to obtain Father's consent to our going to Sydney, for even more than the expense and the inculcation of Theosophical doctrine, he minded Mr Leadbeater, of whom he had a profound mistrust; but he gave way in the end. I do not know what arguments Mother used, but they were certainly weighted by Miss Dodge's offering to pay all our fares, and also to pay for Helen and Ruth to go with us. We would not, however, be travelling with Father to India. As a government official he was obliged to go by P. & O. while we decided to go from Venice by an Italian line because it was cheaper.

We started off from London on October 28, quite a small party this time, consisting of Mother, Betty and me, Krishna, Nitya, Rama Rao, Helen and Ruth. We spent three days in Venice at the Luna Hotel. I was deeply unhappy. Unrequited love was misery enough, but I also felt a hypocrite and a fraud. I had come to realise during those few weeks in London how false my spiritual aspirations were. When the idea of our going to Sydney was first mooted I had unashamedly jumped at it as a means of remaining with Nitya for as long as possible, but I did believe that I had undergone a profound change at Pergine and that to serve the Masters had really become my sole aim in life. Now I knew it was all a sham; and yet I could not back out of it; nor did I wish to. I still wanted to go to Sydney because Nitya was going there.

It was intensely cold, foggy and dismal in Venice, but even so I found it achingly romantic. In spite of the weather an Italian tenor sang *Funiculi, Funicula* beneath my window each night, which hurt me so much that I had to put my head under the bedclothes. I discovered how much harder a heartache is to bear in romantic surroundings. Surely this, of

124

all cities, was intended for happy love? Would I ever know happiness here? (Yes, but I should have to wait twenty-two years for it.) Poor Betty who shared a room with me suffered dreadfully from my reiterated longing for death. Now that my great secret had been offered up I no longer minded showing my feelings to her and must have looked as doleful as I felt when we were alone together.

We sailed on the *Pilsna*, a beautiful small ship of the Lloyd Triestino Line, spotlessly clean with shining new white paint. Her only fault was that the chef was apt to send up cooked food, especially birds and pigs, looking as much as possible as if they were still alive, a practice particularly repulsive to our vegetarian susceptibilities. We did not have one rough day, so in spite of being an atrocious sailor I felt well during the whole of the voyage, but for the first few days I was as wretched as I had been in Venice. Then suddenly my misery turned to indignation. It had seemed to me that, since leaving Pergine, Helen had been trying to captivate Nitya, and the impression was strengthened when we got on board. She was already Krishna's favourite and I greatly resented her trying to win them both. My anger flared up one evening, a few days after we sailed, while we were all sitting together in the saloon after dinner, and I suddenly found myself with the gift of repartee. Nitya and I began to sling arrows of sarcastic wit at each other. It was very exciting, like a long rally at ping-pong. I was probably not nearly as brilliant as I imagined, but brighter than I had ever been before, and certainly bright enough to make an obvious impression on Nitya. His duck had been transformed into a swan as if by magic. And magic I believed it to be. I was convinced that here at last was the return for all those years of unfailingly observing my ritual with the Ranelagh ticket and the foot-mark on the wall. Supernatural aid had come to me at the moment I needed it most.

I could see that Nitya was pleased with me, and this made me pleased with myself and suddenly confident. Confidence must have further enhanced my personality, and as the blood rushed to my head from excitement I have no doubt that my usual pasty appearance was also altered for the better.

I do not know how many days it was after this, but it was

certainly after we got into warm waters and the officers had come out in white ducks, that leaning side by side on the rail of the deck one evening, watching the sunset, Nitya told me that he loved me. He did not kiss me but he held my hand against his heart, and I reached the summit of human happiness.

He told me that he had first loved Barbie, then Madame de Manziarly (this was a great shock to me) and then Rosalind. ('When I first saw Rosalind something seemed to break inside me,' he told me.) 'And now there is you,' he said.

Down in my cabin, which I shared with Mother and Betty, I would not let myself go to sleep that night because I did not want to miss a moment of my conscious bliss. Wave upon wave of ecstasy broke over me. Straight was my path of gold now, stretching away dazzlingly to the end of my days. Everything had slipped into place. Nitya loved me and I loved him, and that added up to 'happy ever after'. Because he now loved me, he would want to be with me always, just as I wanted to be with him always. He had only to say the word and it could easily be arranged. He and Krishna always seemed to get what they wanted.

I do not think it even occurred to me that we might marry. Marriage was not my conception of ideal romance. My ideal was to be together always, and I knew that it was love, not marriage, which bound two people together.

I did not tell Mother what had happened, but surely it must be apparent to everyone? Surely my happiness must shine out of me? I could not keep the smile from my lips or the thrilling little pain from rising in my throat.

For the next few days I remained in a state of ecstasy. Every day after tea we met at the same place on deck where I felt I was completely alone with him (I have no idea whether anyone saw us or not) and we would watch the sun go down over the rim of the horizon with a strange green flash and the sky quickly fill with apricot-coloured twilight. And we would meet again on deck after dinner in the starlight. I do not think we talked very much, and we never kissed, but he would put his cheek against mine and all I wanted was the continuance of this voyage into eternity.

One evening he lent me *An Anthology of Modern Verse* chosen by Algernon Methuen, and told me that his favourite poem in

126

it – perhaps one of his favourite poems in the world – was *Prothalamion* by Francis Brett-Young. As soon as I could find a moment alone I turned to this poem and gulped it down. It intoxicated me, for I learnt from it that Nitya shared exactly my own conception of romance, and this must mean that he loved me in just the way I loved him. We thought alike, felt alike, loved alike. I read the poem over and over again until I knew it by heart. I give it here because it meant so much to me, and was so much a part of my mood.

PROTHALAMION*

When the evening came my love said to me:
   Let us go into the garden now that the sky is cool,
The garden of black hellebore and rosemary,
   Where wild woodruff spills in a milky pool.

Low we passed in the twilight, for the wavering heat
   Of day had waned, and round that shaded plot
Of secret beauty the thickets clustered sweet:
   Here is heaven, our hearts whispered, but our
      lips spake not.

Between that old garden and seas of lazy foam
   Gloomy and beautiful alleys of trees arise
With spire of cypress and dreamy beechen dome,
   So dark that our enchanted sight knew nothing
      but the skies

Veiled with a soft air, drench'd in the roses' musk
   Or the dusky, dark carnation's breath of clove:
No stars burned in their deeps, but through the dusk
   I saw my love's eyes and they were brimmed with
      love.

No star their secret ravished, no wasting moon
   Mocked the sad transience of those eternal hours:
Only the soft, unseeing heaven of June,
   The ghosts of great trees, and the sleeping
      flowers.

*By kind permission of Mrs Francis Brett-Young.

For doves that crooned in the leafy noonday now
    Were silent: the night-jar sought his secret
        covers,
Nor even a mild sea-whisper moved a creaking
        bough –
    Was ever a silence deeper made for lovers?

Was ever a moment meeter made for love?
    Beautiful are your closed lips beneath my kiss;
And all your yielding sweetness beautiful –
    Oh, never in all the world was such a night as
        this.

This poem; the swift beauty of the eastern twilight; the
romantic smell of the ship; the glory of our phosphorescent
wake; the low arch of the sky, like a dark tree, with stars so
close and huge that by standing on the ship's rail one could
have disengaged them at a touch – all this contributed to the
magic of my idyll. For those first few days after Nitya told me
that he loved me I walked in paradise. Never since have I
achieved such a state of unalloyed rapture.

On looking back I can recall the ecstasy, but I do not
remember feeling very much closer to Nitya or gaining any
knowledge of his mind. I was too happy to want to communi-
cate. I felt, as in *Prothalamion*, that our hearts whispered but
our lips spake not; and, besides, had we not got the rest of our
lives together in which to talk? (Alas, how much I might have
learnt about him.) About myself I had nothing to tell him
except of my love, for apart from my love there was nothing
of me but potentiality. I was cosmic jelly quickened into life by
the miracle of his word, awaiting the direction of my creator.

But feeling could not be maintained at such a level. It was
inevitable that after the first few days doubt should set in.
Could this last? Nitya began talking to me about my future.
He wanted me to study while I was in India and Sydney, and
eventually go to Cambridge. 'But what of you?' I asked. He
had his work to do in helping Krishna. Krishna was his life.
He was utterly dedicated to him.

I was brought back with a horrible jolt to the reason why I
was on this ship at all – the Masters and the Path, and the

Coming of the Lord. I had written in my diary a few days before, 'Thank goodness that farce is over'; but it was not over. It had scarcely begun. I had also written: 'I want to be done for ever with hypocrisy,' but Nitya did not feel that anything had changed because he now loved me. Love was incidental to the work. He still expected me to strive towards Initiation. Even a Cambridge degree was of value only in so far as it might increase my usefulness to the Lord when he came. Unless I became a disciple there would be no place for me at Nitya's side in the future. Love for us could never be the warm, exclusive human companionship I longed for.

A couple of days before we arrived in Bombay, Nitya told me when we met on deck as usual after tea that he had coughed up blood that morning, but had not yet told Krishna or anyone else about it. I could see that he was very upset, but I did not realise the full significance of what he had told me.

On our last evening he warned me that things would not be the same when we got to Bombay. For one thing he was ill again, and then we would not be able to see so much of each other; but even this warning was lost on me. He begged me that last evening to make use of my time in Sydney, and I made a silent vow that for his sake, if for no other reason, I would take some steps along the Path while I was there. I told him I would never fail him, and he said he knew it and would love me for always and always.

CHAPTER TWENTY

On November 18 we arrived at Bombay, where we were met by many Theosophists, including Mrs Besant, who garlanded us with wreaths of roses and jasmine entwined with silver tinsel ribbon. This habit of greeting and saying goodbye with garlands is one of the most delightful customs of the East; it is so much more convenient to carry flowers round one's neck than in a bouquet. We were touched and delighted to see Swami, our bearer from the year before, waiting on the dock to come back into our service.

We all went to stay with Ratansi for a few days before going to Adyar. It was heaven the first day to be in India with Nitya; to sit cross-legged on the floor of Ratansi's red-tiled kitchen and eat Indian food off large silver platters. There were so many exquisite smells and tastes that I had forgotten from the year before, particularly the flavour of cardamom and the scent of jasmine. It was exciting to see Nitya for the first time in Indian dress – white cotton jodhpurs and a dark *achkan* fastened high at the neck. Later, at Adyar, he wore a white *dhoti* and a long white silk shirt with a folded silk scarf, bordered in red and gold, round his neck. These clothes suited him and Krishna perfectly, and it was deeply satisfying to see them against their true background. I loved India more than ever.

But all too soon I realised what Nitya had meant when he said that things would not be the same. And yet it was not so much *things* that were different; it was he. Either he was shy of showing me any affection in that house, or he had already ceased to love me. Circumstances need not have made this difference. A look, a word, a pressure of the hand would have been enough to reassure me, but he took no special notice of me whatever, and only a few days after that evening on board when he had told me he would love me for always and always, I was crying out in my diary, 'Surely happiness ought to be found in a wonderful human love? Oh, Nitya, Nitya, why can't I come to you and tell you everything? What is the gulf that day by day widens between us? Must I go back to the world of men? I don't know why Christ was ever born or why one should evolve through suffering.'

As soon as we got to Adyar, where we arrived on December 8, I felt comparatively close to him again. We had our own bungalow there this year, and Helen and Ruth stayed with us. It was on the river, quite close to the headquarters building where we had stayed the year before, and Krishna and Nitya had their meals with us. We found Madame de Manziarly at Adyar with her three daughters. They also had their own bungalow, but they often came to meals in our kitchen, where we sat on the floor and ate off banana-leaves. After the evening meal we would lie on the floor in our bare sitting-room and Mother would read aloud to us. I would lie beside Nitya and he would spread over us both his white Kashmir shawl and I would be happy because under cover of the shawl he held my hand against his heart. As we lay there I watched the lizards flick over the whitewashed walls in pursuit of mosquitoes. Or when there was a moon we would sit by the river after supper, and here again I would be content holding Nitya's hand and feeling close to him.

But I saw hardly anything of him in the daytime except at breakfast (our main meal at half-past ten). There was a meeting every morning in Krishna's room, attended by about forty people, when Krishna would talk to us on much the same lines as at Pergine, but Nitya seldom attended these meetings. He was running a temperature and felt increasingly ill in the mornings. It was no longer a secret that his illness had returned. Krishna, though worried, accepted the general optimism, emanating from Mrs Besant, that the Masters would look after him. They knew best and would dictate what he was to do. His life was far too precious to be lost to the Masters' service; his illness was merely a bit of bad *karma* that had to be worked off.

I too accepted this view. It never crossed my mind that he might die. My faith was deeper than I knew. We all had a

131

strange sense of divine protection. Mother, for instance, took no precautions over our health and used no remedies beyond a cold compress round the tummy. None of us had been vaccinated or given any other kind of inoculation before we set off, and no care beyond ordinary cleanliness was taken with our food. We drank unboiled milk, water from the tap, even at railway stations, and ate uncooked vegetables. (Madame de Manziarly behaved in the same way but for a different reason. It was a theory of hers that you could keep healthy in a country only by drinking its water and milk unboiled; it was a better form of immunisation than any inoculation.) Nor, I think, did it occur to anyone that Nitya's disease was contagious. I certainly never gave it a thought, though had I done so it would not have made any difference to me.

Theosophy did not turn us into fatalists exactly – I suppose there has never been a philosophy that so stresses the need and possibility of changing oneself – but it taught us to accept *outside* circumstances as not only inevitable but all for the best in the long run. If we made ourselves useful enough to the Masters they would protect us in all circumstances.

In accordance with Nitya's wishes I wanted to begin some kind of study while we were at Adyar, but Krishna made it quite clear, through Mother, that any individual work, apart from shorthand and typing, was for the present considered selfish (the Masters, it seemed, could use an unlimited number of shorthand-typists); so after the meetings, which were held at seven o'clock and lasted for about an hour, Betty, Ruth, Helen and I, with the three Manziarly girls, would remain on Krishna's verandah addressing envelopes, sorting letters and typing with one finger. In so doing we remained within the radius of Krishna's aura and also that of Mrs Besant who occupied the floor below, and these good influences were considered to be far more rewarding than any work: the envelopes were just thrown in to keep our hands occupied.

After the main meal we rested until it was cool, and then, at about four, we would meet to play volley-ball on one of the tennis-courts in the compound. Terrific games we had, with sometimes as many as fifteen on each side. Nitya never played

132

now but occasionally he would come to the court to watch us and then I would play with all my heart and strength to impress him. At half-past six we had supper, and after supper the only worth-while part of the day began for me. When, as occasionally happened, Nitya felt too ill to come to supper, I was utterly cast down.

Our time at Adyar was running short. The year had turned to 1925. On January 9 we had to leave to spend some weeks with Father in Delhi, while Ruth and Helen went on ahead to Sydney. In March we would be returning to Adyar to pick up Krishna and Nitya for the journey to Australia.

Before I left I felt I must talk to Nitya alone again. We had had no private conversation since that last evening on board, and I hoped that the unsatisfactory nature of our relationship might be cleared up by one good talk. Two days before we left I managed to get him alone for a moment after breakfast and asked him if, and when, I could see him. He told me to come next day at one o'clock to the room on the first floor of the headquarters building, where he rested alone every afternoon.

I went punctually the next afternoon, having first been to the shrine room in another wing of the building to offer up a prayer, but I did not dare go in at first. Everything was quiet and deserted; the latticed doors were shut, and yet I knew he was in there alone because there was only one pair of sandals outside the door and they were his. It took me a quarter of an hour to summon up courage to go in. Would he be expecting me? Would he be asleep? Would he have forgotten he had asked me to come, as on that occasion years ago when he had forgotten that Nanny and I were coming to tea? I felt so little sure of myself; so little sure of my welcome or of his love.

At last, taking off my sandals and leaving them beside his, I went in. The room was dark and cool after the hot glare outside. The shutters opening on to the verandah were loosely closed and I noticed the intense blue of the river through the crack. Nitya, lying on the big *chowki*, greeted me with the words: 'I thought you were never coming.' He could not have said anything to give me a greater uprush of confidence and happiness.

I lay down on the *chowki* beside him and was able to tell him

133

what was puzzling me so much: surely if two people loved each other they wanted to be together as much as possible? He had said he loved me; why then did he not want to be with me always? Why was it *I* who had had to ask to speak to him? Did he not want to be with me?

He said that I must not get such rubbish into my head. When he had to sit by anyone else or talk to anyone else it was a dreadful effort for him. If I had been twenty I would understand. ('But I am not twenty and I do not understand,' I cried afterwards in my diary.) He had warned me that things would be different when we got to India, and now he was ill again into the bargain – much iller than anybody realised. He knew that he ought really to return at once to Europe for treatment, but he did not want to interfere with Krishna's plans. They had decided to go to Sydney before returning to Ojai and had better stick to the arrangement. He would be quite all right when once he got to Ojai again.

I was overwhelmed then by my own selfishness. He was really very ill and I had been thinking only of myself.

I stayed with him for an hour and a half (I do not think we talked very much), and before I left he asked me to come again the next afternoon at the same time.

I went the next afternoon, and this time entered without trepidation. It would be our last conversation for I did not know how long (we were leaving for Calcutta that evening); there was no knowing how things might have changed when I saw him again, and I had made up my mind what I was going to do. And I did it at once, in case my courage failed me. I bent over him and kissed him on the lips, the culmination of all my dreams.

He said, 'You mustn't do that.'

'Why not?'

'Because it leads to other things. You are too young to understand.'

But in spite of his words he kissed me again himself, far more passionately than I had kissed him.

At that moment the door opened and I sprang away from him. It was only a breeze which had blown it open – I could not have shut it properly – but it had broken the spell between us. I felt guilty for the first time, and I think he must have felt so too, for he said, 'I love you, but you had better go.'

And I went at once without a word. I was exultant, though, and glad beyond measure that I had found the courage to do what I had done. I felt that our kiss had put a seal on our love and that now he would never be able to stop loving me.

CHAPTER TWENTY-ONE

On the way to Delhi we stayed a few days in Calcutta, where Father joined us. The glow inside me lasted while we were there. I recalled those kisses over and over again in imagination, and every time I felt the same thrill as I murmured to myself, 'Beautiful are your closed lips beneath my kiss.' I wondered what would have happened if the door had not blown open. What cruel *karma* to have blown it open just at that moment. I did not believe that the 'other things' Nitya had mentioned, of which I had at least an academic understanding, would have occurred, because I did not particularly want them to (no consummation could be more wonderful than a kiss), but we might have gone on kissing for a long time, and also have had the opportunity of vowing that our love would never change. Just as I had been completely satisfied before with holding his hand, so now I wanted nothing beyond the ecstasy of kissing him.

It was more difficult even than the year before to adapt myself to Government House life. I was still neither fish nor fowl. At sixteen I was not 'out', and yet I felt fully mature compared to my cousin, Davina, much as I loved her. Moreover I was more conscious than ever of Father's apparent dislike of me and boredom in my company. I had always been afraid of boring him, and the sense of constraint I had when I was with him made it almost impossible for me to talk to him naturally. I felt I ought to be amusing and gay and did not know how to be. (My heart still sinks when I am told I am going to meet someone 'amusing' at a party.)

But one very pleasant interlude while we were in Calcutta was a visit we paid to the Institute of Sir Jagadis Chunder Bose, the naturalist, who showed us some of his experiments. These made a deep impression on me and were later to be borne out by some of the strange things about nature which Mr Leadbeater told us. To start with, the Professor revived some dying plants by introducing a solution of his own invention into their water. In a couple of minutes the leaves uncurled in front of our eyes and the plants became upright, fresh and green. Next he demonstrated an apparatus for measuring the heartbeats of flowers, for he maintained that all plants have hearts very much like our own. He showed us a plant registering a normal heartbeat, and then, as we watched, he administered a few drops of poison and we could see on the chart the agonised effort the heart was making to go on beating. After wild fluctuations it grew very faint and finally stopped. He told us that in the course of his experiments he had discovered that some plants become greatly excited in the presence of certain people and their hearts begin to beat at a tremendous rate. (I thought, 'How I should love to be the kind of person who makes the heart of a flower beat faster.') We were next taken into a dark room where a circling play of vivid colours was thrown on to the wall by some kind of projector. The Professor then blew down a wooden pipe but without any effect. He tried a second pipe, with a louder note, and the whole circle of colour vibrated and changed, eventually resuming its original form. We were also shown an experiment which registered the vibrations of an iron rod when a hand was passed in front of it. Until I met Mr Leadbeater I do not remember ever seeing a happier looking man than Professor Bose.

The day we arrived in Delhi, Mother received a letter from Krishna saying that Nitya had taken a turn for the worse and had gone up to Ootacamund in the Nilgiri Hills with Madame de Manziarly and Yo, and that it was unlikely they would now be able to travel with us to Sydney, but would join us there later. This news killed any lingering wish of mine to go to Sydney. It was too late, though, to draw back, not because of any pressure that might have been put on me, but because there was no alternative – and, besides, they would be joining us there, which was still something to live for. But could I not somehow manage to stay behind and travel with Nitya? I wrote to him begging him to let me come and nurse him. He had only to say that he wanted me and it could be managed, and if not I would come anyway; he had only to say the word.

I was not particularly jealous of Madame de Manziarly – it is difficult when you are very young to be jealous of a middle-aged woman – yet it seemed wrong that anyone but I should nurse him. I think I would have stolen money and run away if he had said he wanted me and I had not been allowed to go.

I had no idea that I was making a preposterous suggestion in offering to go and nurse him, and the whole month we were at Delhi I waited for an answer to my letter. I told myself that it would come when things became unbearable, and every morning when I woke to another bleak, blank day, I thought, 'How right it was not to come yesterday. Everything is much worse today. It will surely come today.' But as post followed post and there was still no letter I became increasingly wretched. Forces had been released in me which I could not manage or control, and for which I had no outlet, and when my body got the better of me I loathed myself.

We had some young people to stay but they were no consolation, nor were the various activities with which I sought to kill the time between posts – shorthand and Hindustani lessons, attending sessions of the Legislative Assembly, shopping in the bazaars in old Delhi, getting some clothes made for Sydney (our *derzi* sat on the floor of the verandah and used his toes as much as his fingers to sew with), and watching the building of Father's new city. Except for a few disjointed entries I did not even write in my diary.

Mrs Besant stayed with us for part of the time, but she was very busy with political affairs and I saw little of her. When I did see her, however, I was temporarily released from my torment. I could not help but take on a slight reflection of her greatness. She gave me the impression that she really had reached the end of her evolution and yet had retained a deep understanding of the perplexities and stupidities of mankind. Her smile and her eyes were so radiantly sympathetic. I longed to pour out my heart to her but never quite dared. I believe she might have helped me if I could have told her everything. I did have one talk to her, though, about my future. I asked her whether it was really the wish of the Masters that I should do no individual work, seeing that only the year before she had recommended books for me to study.

138

She replied that to be with Mr Leadbeater in Sydney was a unique opportunity and that I should put myself in his hands and abide by what he told me to do. His methods of training were different from hers, but as I was going to him it was his wishes that must be studied. I wrote in my diary, 'She was angel kind and I adore her more and more and yet once more.' She is the only person in my life for whom I have felt hero-worship, which again is something very different from in-loveness.

Betty, I think, was happy in Delhi. She had taken over the management of the house, which she did extremely well – far better than Mother who was always bored by housekeeping. Like Father, Betty loved people and was an excellent hostess. Poor Father, I have since discovered how much he disliked having Mrs Besant to stay that winter. It must have been a gloomy time for him, and a great contrast from the year before when Ursula and Patsy and the Barings had been there to make it gay for him (probably the happiest winter of all the twenty he spent in Delhi). He so loved gaiety. He liked the house to be constantly full of people, so long as they were people he could joke with. He could not bear the 'hush hush' and 'church all day feeling', as he described it, which surrounded Mrs Besant. We never spent an evening *en famille* in Delhi. If there was no one else to invite, he would ask a couple from the office. He had designed a large round blackboard top for the dining-room table and each guest was provided with a piece of chalk laid out ceremoniously beside the knives. Many a sticky moment was relieved by a game of noughts and crosses, or, in Father's case, by enchanting drawings. Especially was the chalk useful when Indian ladies just out of purdah came to dinner and could not open their mouths without instinctively covering the lower part of their faces with their napkins. Mother had a way of sitting on one of her own feet at dinner and more than once fell to the floor when she got up.

It has been said of Father that he joked to cover his shyness. That may have been true in his early days but by now it had become a habit and some of his jokes were mere reflexes. For instance, he could never see a dish of butter without exclaiming, 'Butter late than never.' It was at a dinner party in

Delhi that he made a joke which has been quoted as one of his best. A very shy young man called Mr Weston came to dinner and Father suddenly asked him in a loud voice across the table, 'Are you any relation to the Great Western?'

'I don't think so, sir,' the young man replied seriously, and then he blushed as everyone laughed and, too late, he saw the joke. Father had not meant to be unkind but he could not have intended either, as has been suggested, to put him at his ease. Mr Weston had merely been the victim of a joke, and I felt deeply sorry for him when I heard this story, because I myself was never sure when I might not be such a victim. It was all right if one was very quick-witted, but I was not, and too often I saw the joke too late and was made to feel a fool. One of Father's perennial parlour-tricks was to ask a newcomer to take hold of two matches protruding from a closed matchbox, and, having first asked him whether he was afraid of electric shocks, say, 'Now raise your right leg slightly. Do you feel your leg being pulled?'

But some of his oft-repeated stories I was never tired of hearing. My favourite was about a bishop who went to stay away from Saturday to Monday, and when on Saturday evening he was pressed by his hostess to say what he would like for breakfast next morning, a wide choice being given to him (Father would here enumerate as many orthodox breakfast dishes as he could think of), replied unhesitatingly, 'I would like owls' bowels on toast.'

Another cherished story needed a pack of cards for its telling: a farmer had been out until nightfall looking for his lost cows, and just as he was about to abandon the search until the next morning because it was too dark to see, he heard . . . And here Father would drop the cards in driblets on to some hard surface.

He could not pronounce his R's and always called me Mawy, and usually his 'little Mawy', rubbing his tummy. When he felt affectionate he would put his arms round me and sway from side to side singing, 'Lead us, gentle Shepherd, lead us.' (He had a distinctive but pleasant smell somewhat reminiscent of the wood-shavings of a pencil.) This was very endearing and I always welcomed the gentle shepherd treatment, just as I welcomed it when he played on my

140

vertebrae as on the stops of a flute, but at other times, without warning, he would make some devastating personal remark which hurt or embarrassed me to the point of hating him. Once, when someone remarked that I was like his mother, he protested sharply, 'Oh, *no*, Mother was *beautiful*,' and he said it in so unqualified a way that it took from me all moral as well as physical pretensions to beauty.

It was probably because I was so proud of him and of his work that I was so sensitive to his criticism. His taste was my law. I took on all his aesthetic prejudices and most of his other prejudices as well. Among these were a dislike of long-stemmed glasses (even our wine and port glasses at home were designed without stems, like shallow tumblers); fish-knives; cut flowers; silk lamp-shades; pile carpets (if a floor must be close-carpeted let it be haircord); the seaside; the placing of furniture diagonally; painted nails and the putting of any kind of instrument under the nails to clean them, even the bristles of a nail-brush. He maintained that a nail should fit closely over the finger like the skin of an almond. His mother's nails had fitted so. His too were skin-like and beautifully shaped, but there was a permanent black rim under them which he never attempted to remove. Moreover, he would often use his fingers as an indiarubber, and one of the things which surprised me most in his unlikeness to myself was that he could bear always to have such dirty hands.

Another prejudice of his was against statistics, and he would give this example to illustrate how ridiculously mis-leading they could be: a fatal new disease had come into existence, the average age at which it struck down its victims being forty-six. On investigation it was found that there had been two deaths from this disease, a child of two and an old man of ninety.

In Delhi that winter I made my one and only attempt to draw him out in conversation. I asked him how he had managed to become an architect without ever going to school, something I really wanted to know. He grunted and replied grumpily without looking up or taking his pipe out of his mouth or ceasing to deal cards for his Patience, 'All you've got to know is that water runs down hill, and any fool knows that,' and he said it so as not only to close the conversation but to

141

make me feel that it was the stupidest possible question to have asked. This reply of his was rather like his panacea, 'Go and make boots,' which ever since I could remember I had heard him apply to almost every problem under consideration, and by which I understood him to mean, 'Go and acquire a manual skill.'

As one grows older one comes to understand one's parents. They reveal themselves in letters which are read only after their death, and then there is a heartbreaking realisation that one was, after all, dear to them. How unhappy Father must have been to see Betty and me being ruined, as he thought, and he powerless to enforce his authority without risking a break-up of his home. There was no real contact between us; but was it not perhaps for him to try to get to know me? If I were not close to my own child I should look for the fault in myself. And yet what point of contact could he have had with me? Even if he had tried to win my confidence, which he never did, he was the last person I could have confided in. He could not be expected to sympathise with our avowed reason for going to Sydney, and had he known my true reason he would have been appalled and no doubt have insisted on taking me back with him to England, thereby depriving me of some invaluable experience.

Ursula was the only one of us who did not at any time come under the influence of Theosophy, and I am inclined to think that this was because Father had established a special relationship with her almost from the time she was born. If he had earlier won my love, when it could so easily have been won, I might have complied with his wishes, but in that case I would have missed Sydney and probably Theosophy altogether, which would have been a great waste, for however damaging and painful at the time those influences were which led me to Sydney, I would not have missed the experience for the world. Although it has immunised me against all isms, organisations, societies and communal activities, which may or may not be a good thing, it has, I like to think, given me balance, a respect for the beliefs of others, however strange, and a sense of proportion.

Even at that time I was aware of Father's feelings, for I knew him much better than he knew me. I wrote in my diary in the train on our way back to Madras: 'Poor Father was so upset when Mummie went. I pity him, and, in a way, admire him from the bottom of my heart. He works and slaves from dawn till dark and we spend his money on the things he loathes. And to make matters worse, Delhi, his life's work, is already crumbling before his eyes,' and I went on to describe the bad materials and bad workmanship employed by a stingy Government, who refused to raise the standard of Indian labour by paying fair wages, and the resentment of the Indians themselves against this new capital which was not on the site they would have chosen – three closely-written pages of fulmination against the British Raj.

CHAPTER TWENTY-TWO

Betty and I were both ill on the journey back to Adyar, and after we arrived there on February 20 we had to take to our beds with the inevitable cold compress, but on that day, when I least expected it, my letter came. Even then I was not accorded the joy of an envelope to myself. It came enclosed in a letter to Mother – two sheets of flimsy paper folded in four with Mary written on the outside in Nitya's careful round writing that was so like Krishna's. (Both their writings were strongly imitative of Mr Leadbeater's.) I have it still – the paper discoloured and torn at the creases and the pencil writing so faint that I can hardly read it – but what does that matter, for I know it by heart?

Gulistar, Ooty, Feb. 19.25

My dearest Mary,

Please forgive my not writing to you before, but so far, writing a letter has meant a rise in my fever, and also I've been too feeble to write. But in the last week I've been much better, and now I'm on my way to recovery, Sydney and Ojai. I've been in bed for four weeks and my bones are wearing through my skin. The number of times I walk to the precipice of death, look over and walk back again! It is becoming a habit with me. When I really do die at the mature age of 90 or so, I shall by force of habit continue to live.

My days consist of superb inactivity. I pass from one book to another, forgetting the last page as I read the next; but it's been the worst four weeks I've ever spent. To feel ill, feeble and a failure is a horrible combination.

How was Delhi, Mary, and how are you? I think you and I need to pray for strength and nothing else. For God's sake and for my sake make use of your stay in Sydney. I shall see you there in a little over six weeks. But whatever you do or don't do, I shall always love you, but you will do great things and be great, Mary, you have it in you and don't waste it. 'From those to whom great gifts are given great deeds are demanded.'

With all my love,
Nitya.

I realised that after all the letter had come at the perfect moment, when I must begin to think of what lay ahead in Sydney. Its sweetness released me from my torment and left me free to consider the future. He expected great things of me (I have never discovered where that quotation came from) and I must not fail him. Why did he look upon himself as a failure? I could not understand it. Surely it must be merely a figure of speech. In what conceivable way had he failed? By getting ill again?

I had not given a thought to my spiritual aspirations during those miserable weeks in Delhi, and now Nitya's letter brought home to me the imminence of Sydney, and I was terrified. How unready I was for this great opportunity. The Masters had never seemed so unreal. A letter from Helen in Sydney, sounding gloriously happy, came by the same post as Nitya's; and this was another frightening reminder of how soon we were to be plunged into that unknown world. I was glad now that Krishna and Nitya would not be coming with us. If I did not see Nitya again before we left, and if he did nothing further to hurt me, I could go as a freeman. I *could* not go in bondage.

I did not answer his letter, although he had asked me how I was, because I did not want to live again through the hell of waiting for an answer, and the precious letter I had received I could feed on until I next saw him: it brought me a rush of happiness every time I read it, which was about a dozen times a day. 'Whatever you do or don't do, I shall always love you.' It was the only assurance I needed.

It was wonderful to emerge from the fog of self-absorption. Never had Adyar looked more beautiful, and it was lovely, too, to be near Krishna again.

To raise money for the Star we put on three short plays in the next couple of weeks. Mar de Manziarly and I wrote and stage-managed them, and I was able to throw myself into this activity with my whole being, and was thrilled when Mrs Besant asked me after the performance why I did not take up acting as a career. Twice now my acting had been praised (the first time by Nitya at Boissy), and it was very pleasant to think of myself as a potential actress, though how the Masters could use me in that capacity I had no idea.

The only source of disquiet during those days at Adyar was a letter from Nitya to Rosalind, which he had sent to Mother to deliver to her in Sydney. (It may be remembered that Rosalind had gone to Sydney when Krishna and Nitya returned to England the previous July.) This letter, which was in a closed envelope, Mother kept on her dressing-table, where it was a constant temptation to me. If I could have opened it without detection, I should certainly have done so.

And then I heard to my dismay that our departure was to be put off for a fortnight, so that we might travel with Krishna and Nitya after all.

Nitya was to come down from Ootacamund on March 11, and on the 10th I wrote in my diary: 'My God, do I have to go back into slavery to-morrow? I will, will fight against it. I loathe that feeling of having no will – no individuality of my own – going about all day with a lump in my throat and crying myself to sleep. To-morrow will it all come back again – jealousy, wild longing, a miserable ache inside – and a body which gets beyond my control? My God, it shall not be.'

But it was to be worse than anything I could have imagined.

I had expected to see Nitya as soon as he arrived, but a message came to me through Mother to say that he was too ill to see anyone. We were leaving next day for Colombo – just Mother, Betty, Krishna, Nitya and I – but at the last moment Jinarajadasa, one of the leaders of the Theosophical Society, decided to come with us to look after Nitya. (He was said to be Leadbeater's murdered brother, speedily reincarnated.)

I did not so much as catch a glimpse of Nitya on the journey to Colombo. We had different compartments on the train and he had a cabin on the boat to Ceylon. My first sight of him was when we got on board the *Ormuz* and had to stand in line for passport inspection. He looked appallingly ill. He smiled at me, and Mother comforted me a little afterwards by saying that his whole face lit up when he saw me. I got no other help from her, although I think she must have been aware of my state of mind to vouchsafe even that amount of comfort. No doubt she reasoned that she had had to struggle alone to sublimate her own feelings for Krishna, and that I must do likewise. Or perhaps it was that seeing me happy at Adyar she imagined I had got over my infatuation, or at least got on top of it.*

Nitya's appearance was a terrible shock to me. His face was hollow; he must have lost several stone in weight and he could obviously hardly stand. He was leaning heavily on Jinaraja-dasa. For the first time I *knew* how ill he was, and this did more than anything to purify the intense selfishness of my love.

If nothing else had happened during that voyage I might have managed to submerge myself in concern for him (I spent the first evening on board quite happily writing out menus for him, at Krishna's dictation, to give to the chef) even though he would not or could not see me (he had all his meals in his own cabin), but a few days after we sailed, Krishna came out at dinner with the news that Rosalind was going to take care of him when we got to Sydney, and that after the mere fortnight they intended to spend there she would be returning with them to Ojai as his nurse. I had to fight with myself not to get up from the table. However weak I was inwardly, self-control in public had become second nature to me, but I have never had to struggle harder to maintain it. I am sure Krishna knew better than anyone what this meant to me, for I had had one talk with him when we got back to Adyar, when I had confessed that I wanted to nurse Nitya and he had told me not to be a damned fool; but the news had to be broken, and doubtless he felt that this was the best way of breaking it.

That night in my bunk above Mother I opened a penknife and pressed it against my wrist, longing for the courage to slash the blue veins I could see just under the skin, but I was afraid of blood. I could imagine it dripping over the edge of my bunk on to the floor (how long would it be before Mother noticed it?)

*Mother has now read this book and declares that she had no idea of my feelings for Nitya. Indeed she believed my devotion to be wholly given to Krishna.

and this made me feel faint. But if I had had at my disposal some easier way out of life, such as sleeping pills, I have no doubt I should have taken it. I did not see how I could go on living with this new anguish, or how I could now face Sydney.

That voyage was particularly hard, for it was impossible not to compare it with the journey on the *Pilsna*. I discovered that there is nothing so hurting as the remembrance of dead happiness; and *War and Peace*, which I was reading for the first time (leaving out the war bits which bored me), was like salt on my raw heart. It was too unjust that Natasha, who had betrayed Prince Andrew in the most heartless way, should nurse him on his deathbed, while I, who had been faithful to Nitya all these years, should not even be allowed to see him. I was outraged by the injustice of it; but in the end when the terrible fate of marrying that dreary Peter overtook Natasha and she was dragged down into the sordidness of domesticity, I forgave her somewhat, principally, I think, because she had lost all her charm.

I do not know how long it was before I discovered where Nitya lay all day on deck, but directly I did discover it, quite by chance, I spent a great part of my time watching him. Standing at a port-hole in one of the alleyways, I could see him clearly, a little to the left and in front of me, in a deck-chair facing out to sea with a rug over his knees. He wore a dressing-gown, and there was always a book on his lap, but he was seldom reading, just staring straight ahead of him with an expression I could not see, although I could see that his eyes were open. He kept incredibly still, and so did I at my spy-hole, moving only if someone came along the alleyway, or if Jinarajadasa or Krishna appeared on deck to speak to him, or the steward to bring him a tray.

I was tortured by the temptation to go to him. It would have been so easy – just out of the door and along the deck. I could pretend I had come across him by chance, and give a start of surprise when I saw him. (I might really have come across him by chance if I had not happened to see him first through the port-hole.) But I could no more find the courage to go to him than to cut my wrist. Each night I vowed I would go to him next day, and each day I determined to finish myself off that night. I was as near one as the other. If I had

148

been brave enough to go to him and he had snubbed me, I believe I would have been desperate enough to let out my blood.

Natasha had gone to Prince Andrew at their first halting-place on the flight from Moscow, so why could not I go to Nitya? Was it not her courage that had given her the right to nurse him? But I knew that however brave I was I would not be given that right. Nitya knew I loved him. It was for him to ask for me. Prince Andrew had not known what Natasha's feelings were, and only she could enlighten him. Our circumstances were exactly opposite, and I could not have felt more bitterness against her if she had been a personal enemy. I had not yet come to her sordid marriage, and my jealousy of her was at its peak. I felt no sympathy for her when Prince Andrew died. What was his death, knowing that he loved her, compared to the agony of my own situation?

As I stood watching Nitya, sometimes for hours on end, I wondered and wondered what was going on in his head, and felt that if I willed hard enough I might be able to get inside his mind. Surely he must have had some awareness of the fierce concentration I used to penetrate his thoughts, but not once did he turn his head in my direction or seem in any way conscious of a watching presence.

How little I ever really knew him, even in those few hours of twilight on board the *Pilsna*. He was never very real to me except for the misery and joy he caused me, which were real enough. I was never able to see him objectively, apart from those few days in Vienna, and even from this distance of more than thirty years I can still look at him only through the haze of my old emotions. I was so puzzled by what had happened; I could not understand it. I did not know why he had changed, why he would not see me, or what I had done to deserve this anguish. Such a short time ago he had written that he would love me always: then why, why, why would he not see me? Bewilderment was a large part of my misery. If only I could have talked to someone who would explain the mystery to me. What was the mystery? I knew from his letter that he was unhappy too; then why could we not comfort each other?

Poor Nitya, I do not think he can ever have been very

149

happy. He had always been obliged to play second fiddle to Krishna. Nothing in his life was ever completed; nothing ever reached fulfilment. His illness came to interrupt his studies for the Bar, though it is unlikely in the strange existence he and Krishna led, always subject to the whims of the Masters as made known through their interpreters, that he would have been allowed to practise, for it is unthinkable that he would ever have broken away from Krishna. And yet how often with one side of his nature he must have longed to escape, and direct his energies into normal channels, for he was not a natural mystic like Krishna. He had brains, character and charm; great affections and certainly latent passion. How India alone needed his talents.

It was more in the early days, though, that he must have longed to escape. His whole outlook, as well as Krishna's, had been changed by Krishna's spiritual awakening at Ojai in 1922. Something very extraordinary had happened then of which I knew none of the details. It was not until about two months later that Mother read to Betty and me the beautiful accounts of this experience which both Krishna and Nitya had written at the time and which were circulated among a few trusted people, including Mother and Miss Dodge. I wish I had read them sooner, because, when I did, they helped me more than anything to understand and accept Nitya's life of dedication. (If only Mother had read them to me on board, what a difference it might have made.) And I wish I could obtain permission to include here at least Nitya's account of what happened,* because it brings him to life as no words of mine can do, and I so long to give him immortality.

But I imagine that during the time I watched him day after day through the port-hole, his chief concern was with his health, and all his energies concentrated on getting well. He knew that he ought to have gone straight back to Europe, and that his life was being risked. Did he really believe that he was on the road to recovery? Perhaps he felt my miserable presence behind him day after day and mistook it for the spectre of death.

*Both Nitya's and Krishna's accounts of the experience at Ojai in 1922 are published in *Krishnamurti: The Years of Awakening* by Mary Lutyens (Rider, 1984).

I never found the courage to go to him, so I shall never know how he would have received me; and I was still in the same state of wretched, bewildered indecision when we arrived in Sydney.

CHAPTER TWENTY-THREE

There was a crowd to meet us when we docked at Sydney on the morning of April 3. With the exception of Nitya we were all on deck to watch our entrance into the famous harbour. Knowing that Mr Leadbeater was likely to meet us, I endeavoured to fill my mind with beautiful images, for I knew that through clairvoyance he could see our auras, which were constantly changing colour according to our thoughts and feelings, the base passions such as anger, jealousy, lust and so on, turning them flaming red or an ugly muddy tone. What was the use of washing one's face and hands and brushing one's hair, only to be given away by a dirty aura? I had hoped that the beauty of the harbour might help me to cleanse my aura, and was particularly disappointed, therefore, to find its shores defaced with gasometers and other hideosities.

As we drew alongside I picked out Mr Leadbeater at once. He came prancing down the wharf like a great lion, hatless and in a long purple cloak, holding on to the arm of a very good-looking blond boy of about fifteen. One could not have failed to notice him in any crowd, even apart from his dress, for not only was he very tall but the hair of his uncovered head was snow-white and he had a long white beard.

He came on board and we were introduced to him and to the fair boy, an Australian called Theodore St John. Then Bishop (for we discovered that Leadbeater was now always called by his title), Mother, Betty and I went down to the dining saloon, where we sat on swivel-chairs at a bare table and talked for about twenty minutes. Bishop had the merriest of twinkling blue eyes, a jolly manner and a very loud though pleasant voice. I was immediately impressed by his air of sparkling health, as if every faculty, mental and physical, was kept in perfect working order for immediate use. His teeth, although very white and apparently without decay, and certainly his own, were exceptionally long and pointed (all his visible teeth were like that, not just his eye teeth) so that the word vampire jumped to my mind. Under his cloak he wore a red cassock with a large amethyst cross dangling at the breast, and on the third finger of his right hand a huge amethyst ring.

The impact of his personality was like a plunge into cold water. It shocked and braced me. He was seventy-eight, but apart from his white hair might have been a much younger man. If he had not been a great spiritual teacher he would undoubtedly have been great at something else. He gave me the feeling that there was *nothing* he would not do or dare. Now I had met him I could easily believe the chamber-pot story, and all the other strange tales I had heard about him too, but not the accusation of immorality. He looked far too healthy and happy to be abnormal.

He began to talk to us at once, sitting there in the empty dining saloon, of what he called the 'real things', and asked Betty and me point-blank whether we were prepared to offer ourselves to the Masters' service. We said we were. When the noise outside became too great he put his hands to his mouth and shouted through them as through a megaphone.

By the time we went back on deck Krishna and Nitya had gone, and I was glad of it, for I could not have answered for the state of my aura if I had had to witness Nitya's meeting with Rosalind. I heard that she had met them, but I did not see her. My heart was dreadfully sore when I thought of them together. She was going to look after him day after day, and he would not even see me. He and Krishna were not going to stay with us at the Manor, but at a house close by, Myola, with a middle-aged Scotch couple called Mackay, who, though devotees of Leadbeater, kept their own establishment, and Rosalind was going to stay there with them.

We motored with Bishop to the Manor at Mosman, one of the suburbs of Sydney. (Normally when we went into town from Mosman we took the ferry, but today we had luggage.) It was a day of bewildering impressions. First there was the Manor itself, a huge and hideous villa built by a millionaire in the vain hope that his married children and their families

153

would come and live there with him. He had been his own architect and had for some unexplained reason lined most of the rooms with beaten copper. This was ideal for Bishop's purpose, because copper, we were told, conserved magnetism, and he had therefore been able to put all sorts of good influences into the house. Mother, Betty and I were to share a room on the ground floor, and I think all our hearts sank when we saw it. There were three iron bedsteads, one small chest of drawers between the three of us and a few hanging pegs. But as a compensation it was next to Bishop Leadbeater's own room, so that we would come directly under his influence, and, like his room, it opened on to a verandah flanking the house on the sea side, with a wonderful view over the harbour.

Then there were the inmates whom we met at lunch. They took a good deal of sorting out. There were fifty-two of them (fifty-five with us) of many nationalities and all ages – some living in single rooms and some sharing larger rooms like ourselves. There were women with their children (there was even a baby) and a few married couples, but the majority were girls and boys unrelated to each other, between the ages of nine and twenty-five. At first sight they all seemed a bit dreary and mediocre; badly dressed and uncouth.

The dining-room was in the basement and, as in a school, contained three long trestle tables for the inmates, while Bishop, like a headmaster, presided at a small table set at right angles to the other three and raised above them on a dais. We helped ourselves from a large sideboard, as in a cafeteria, our first experience of self-service. The food was, of course, vegetarian but extremely good and very plentiful. Meals, however, were an ordeal because Bishop could not stand noise, and the effort of fifty-five people trying to eat soundlessly was a cumulative nerve-strain. A knife dropped or a plate clattered would draw on the culprit a stern look from the dais. Silence was not enforced but we talked little and then only in whispers.

There was already a severe servant-shortage in Sydney and the few maids we could get worked only an eight-hour day. We had to do our own room, therefore, clean our own shoes and clean out the bath after we had used it. (There was a bath

154

opposite our room but it was shared by the whole of the ground floor, which was given over to bedrooms, and we were put on a rota for its use.) As neither Mother, Betty nor I had ever done a hand's turn for ourselves, we found these chores very irksome, particularly as we were so slow and inefficient. There was a gas-ring in our room, on which we boiled water for our tea and hot water bottles. We also had supper in our own room because only breakfast and lunch were provided in the dining-room, and we washed up afterwards in a sink at the end of the corridor.

We paid a weekly sum for our board and lodging. I have forgotten how much, although I took charge of our finances after Mother left. A Dutchman looked after the financial affairs of the Manor. We paid according to our means, and Mother was no doubt looked upon as being very rich, though the Dutchman was the richest of us all. We certainly spent a great deal while we were there, and twice Mother was obliged to cable to Father for funds, which were promptly sent. There is a later entry in my diary in which I say that I have added up the counterfoils in Mother's cheque-book from April 6 to May 12 and find she had paid out £194.10.11, which seemed to me 'a colossal sum'.

The very afternoon of our arrival, Bishop Leadbeater took Mother, Betty and me into his room, which was lined from floor to ceiling with copper beaten into strange and hideous designs, and talked to us for over an hour, with great courtesy and sweetness, about the Masters and what it meant to follow them. He said there was no compulsion to follow them because we would all arrive in the end at the goal of Perfection, whether we strove for it or not, but that for those of us who wished to travel faster along the Path so as to help humanity in its upward evolution there were the Masters whose pupils we could become. Apprenticeship, he said, was really a better word than pupil, for a pupil need not follow his master's calling, whereas an apprentice was trained to do so. He then talked to us of the nature of God. He said that the Monad was the divine spark in each one of us which put down into levels lower than its own a partial manifestation of itself called the ego. This unfolded its latent divine qualities through many successive lives in a still lower world, in the

155

course of which it clothed itself in vehicles suitable to that world, to which we gave the name of body. While the ego was reaching upward, that which composed the bodies was descending lower into matter. Therefore all our bad feelings were not temptations of the devil, as was commonly supposed, but our lower selves continuing on the line of their own evolution. Some people had been foolish enough to say that if we gave way to our bad instincts we should thereby be helping on their evolution, but in truth, if the lower self was starved, it would soon drop out and take up its abode in the body of some passing dog or cat where its appetite would be more easily satisfied.

I went to bed that night with a sense of despair. Nitya was with Rosalind and I did not know when, if ever, I should see him again. I felt I was going to hate our new life and the ugliness of everything. Our beds were very close together and the coarse, brand-new cotton sheets, still full of dressing, made a horrible crackling sound every time we turned over. Towards morning I dreamt that Nitya had turned into a white kitten and I was holding him in my arms, where he nestled contentedly. I woke sobbing with the feel of his soft fur still against my neck, but quickly controlled myself as I recollected that Bishop was next door and could probably hear every sound as well as read my thoughts. He was so like my early conception of God.

That afternoon he called us into his room again and told Betty and me that we were to choose between the two Masters who held the Theosophical Society under their special protection – the Master Morya and the Master Koot Hoomi (a reincarnation of Pythagoras) – who lived on either side of a narrow valley in Tibet. We were shown their portraits, painted by Mrs St John, Theodore's mother, from memories on the astral plane. We both chose the Master Koot Hoomi, whose picture, we were told, bore a striking likeness to him. Bishop said he would take us that night on the astral about midnight to the house of Master Koot Hoomi and obtain his approval of us as potential candidates for discipleship. He asked us if we slept well, and when I replied that Betty was a poor sleeper, he said, 'Well, if she isn't asleep by midnight we'll just have to wait around for her.' Theodore St John, who was psychic, then drew for us a plan of the Master's house from astral memory, so that we might feel more at home when we got there.

As a matter of fact it was I who was so long in going to sleep that night that I was afraid I should be left behind when the others set off for Tibet, but a cough from Bishop on the other side of the wall reassured me that he, too, was still awake.

We remembered nothing, but were happy to be told next morning that the Master Koot Hoomi had approved of us.

CHAPTER TWENTY-FOUR

The only people we knew at the Manor were Helen and Ruth, Ruth's mother Mrs Roberts, her younger sister Monica, and Mrs Roberts's sister, Dr Mary Rocke, who was an old friend of Mother's from her early Theosophical days.

Theodore St John was Bishop's favourite pupil at the moment. He was an Initiate and a high-spirited boy who radiated good nature, but he was a little too jaunty for my liking, though not quite to the point of bumptiousness. He had become great friends with Ruth since she had been there, and he now took Betty up, and the three of them, with Helen sometimes to make a fourth, formed a little coterie who went bathing together every day in a sea-pool at Mosman, shut off from sharks by wire-netting. But as well as a love of swimming (Betty was like a fish in the water, whereas I could never do more than a slow and solemn breast-stroke), Theodore and Betty had music in common. He played the violin and the piano. Helen also played the violin, so the three of them had regular sessions. It made all the difference to Betty to be taken up by Theodore, and consequently she was much happier in Sydney during the eight months we were there than I was; but it was certainly her turn to be favoured. She had not been happy at Ehrwald or Pergine, where she had felt that I was preferred.

The atmosphere of the Manor had such a bewildering force that for the first few days, until we got accustomed to it, it was like being blind and deaf inside a power station. In spite of the enforced quiet at meals, one felt shaken and stupefied by unseen, unheard vibrations.

I had not intended to take any part in the activities of the Liberal Catholic Church, of which Leadbeater was Regionary Bishop for Australasia; but it was made clear to us on the very

158

first day that if we did not join that Church we might just as well not have come to Sydney, as it was one of the main channels used by the Masters to pour their influence through us. There was a chapel in the basement at the Manor where Mass was celebrated every morning before breakfast, and Vespers and Benediction services held every evening. We attended Vespers and Benediction on the evening of our arrival. Most of the men and boys living at the Manor were priests, deacons or sub-deacons in the Liberal Catholic Church. We were told that 'this daily Eucharist' was something which practically nobody was given 'outside the Communities of monks and nuns'.

In 1870 a large number of Roman Catholics who would not subscribe to the new dogma of papal infallibility were excommunicated. They organised themselves into congregations and took the name of the Old Catholic Church. Through a Jansenist Bishop of Deventer in Holland they handed on apostolic succession. In 1908 A. A. Mathew was consecrated as Bishop of Great Britain and Ireland. He handed on the succession to Bishop Willoughby, who, in turn, consecrated J. I. Wedgwood in 1916. Wedgwood was a Theosophist. He went to Sydney in the year he became a Bishop and duly consecrated Leadbeater. The name Old Catholic Church was changed to the Old Catholic Mission and finally to the Liberal Catholic Church. Leadbeater and Wedgwood between them wrote a new liturgy for it. It was in English, but the services were much more in accordance with Roman Catholicism than with Anglicanism, except for the hymns which were pure Church of England. (Leadbeater loved singing hymns.) There was no confession, however, probably because the theory of absolution is contrary to the law of *karma*, and the wafer was dipped into the wine before being placed on the communicant's tongue. Mother had become a Liberal Catholic in 1917, and it was a Liberal Catholic priest who had come to Bedford Square to exorcise its evil spirits.

Although I had been baptised, I had not been confirmed in the Church of England, for I had not wanted to be bound by the narrowness of any one Church, but now Betty and I were given no time to think over this great step we were to take. Two days after we arrived in Sydney, on Palm Sunday, April

159

5, we were baptised and confirmed in the new Church and I cared too little to put up any resistance. As I put it in my diary, 'On Palm Sunday Betty and I went the whole hog.'

In the morning we went into town, where the Dutchman who looked after the Manor finances baptised us at the Liberal Catholic Church of St Alban, and after returning to the Manor for lunch (the Sunday lunches at the Manor were really delicious I was to discover) went back to St Alban to be confirmed by Bishop Leadbeater.

I was dreading my confirmation and the embarrassment of walking up to Bishop by myself; and then to add to my self-consciousness Krishna unexpectedly appeared in the church. But when the moment came and I was kneeling before Bishop and had put my hands, palms together, on his lap and spoken the words, 'Right Reverend Father, I offer myself to be a knight in Christ's service,' I lost all shyness and only wanted to go on kneeling there for ever. Bishop took my hands between his and I knew that he knew everything that was going on inside me. It was the most extraordinary sensation of being turned completely inside out like an old pocket; and such power to help myself came to me – whether from him or from some force beyond him I do not know – that from that moment I was able, first to control, and then to exorcise, the devils of the flesh which had been tormenting me.

Betty, as well as joining the Church, became a Co-Mason (another channel for the Masters) but for some unexplained reason this was not thought to be necessary for me, although if I had been told to join by Theodore (Bishop's mouthpiece) I should certainly have done so. The Co-Masons, who admitted women to their Order, had broken away from the French Order in 1881. Mrs Besant had become a Co-Mason in 1902, and through her influence the movement had spread rapidly in several countries.

Krishna had no sympathy with the Church or with Co-Masonry. In fact he was extremely sarcastic about them. (He had a deep aversion to ceremonial of all kinds.) It was not very fair of him, though, to mock our efforts to conform, for after all, it was he who had urged us to come to Sydney and had told us over and over again what a marvellous opportunity it was, and if we had not fallen in with Leadbeater's wishes what was the point of being there? I imagine that when Krishna had been in Sydney three years before, these ceremonies had not played such a large part in the Manor routine, and that it was a shock to him to discover how much of our time was to be devoted to church-going. He presided at a few meetings while he was there and had some long private talks with Lead-beater, but it was a little difficult to understand why he had bothered to come, for he was as out of place in that mediocre community as a gazelle in a flock of sheep, whereas Bishop was as much at home there as the shepherd.

There was one occasion when Krishna made things par-ticularly difficult for me. On Monday evenings a young man called Harold, an Australian, held a meeting in his ground-floor room which we were expected to attend. Harold, who was an Initiate, was Leadbeater's ex-favourite. He had been superseded by Theodore only a short time before we arrived, and had accepted his lowered status with a saintly complaisance, as befitted an Initiate. At the first meeting we went to, the day after Palm Sunday, during the meditation which preceded Harold's talk, while we sat in a circle hold-ing hands and I tried, behind closed lids, to concentrate on my unity with these unloved strangers, I suddenly opened my eyes to see Krishna grinning at me through the window. The sight of him almost undid all the good of my confirma-tion. I was trying so hard, but Krishna standing there outside, laughing and winking, brought back my old pain so overwhelmingly that I did not know how I could go on, how I could bear it. How different was this from Pergine with Krishna talking to us under the apple trees and Nitya lying close beside me on the rug – and yet all Krishna's talk had been directed towards this present, this unique opportunity, this goal of Sydney.

I think he must also have made Ruth and Helen rather miserable while he was there, but they were firmly established at the Manor by the time we arrived, and fundamentally very happy there, so perhaps he did not shake them as he shook me. But I was too self-absorbed to notice much, or care much, what the others were feeling.

About a week after we arrived Krishna went away to the hills with Nitya. On the 7th a specialist had been to see Nitya and pronounced that as well as his left lung being very much worse, his right lung was now also affected. His journey to America would have to be postponed until he was better, and in the meantime he must get away immediately from Sydney to the Blue Mountains. The next day a furnished house was bought for him at Leura, near Katoomba, sixty miles west of Sydney, and there he, Krishna and Rosalind, with Mrs Roberts as chaperone, moved a few days later.

I had seen him only once since we arrived, and that was a mere glimpse through the window from the garden of Myola. He was sitting on the window-sill in his dressing gown, and there was a shadowy figure standing just behind him which I took to be Rosalind. I was with Helen and Betty, and the moment I saw him I began to dance about and shout and laugh. (This behaviour shows me more than anything that I was still a child.) Mrs Mackay came out and asked us to go away as the noise we were making was disturbing Nitya, and this gave me a perverse satisfaction, just as a self-inflicted pinch can momentarily alleviate a deep-seated pain.

There was never any lack of money in our movement for expensive houses or journeys if they were said by our leaders to be necessary. Either appeals were issued, to which the members responded as if their spiritual advancement depended on it, or some rich member, like Miss Dodge, came to the rescue. This time it was Dr Rocke, Mrs Roberts's sister, who bought the house for Nitya at Leura. She was well off and extremely generous. It was also at her expense that an outdoor amphitheatre was being constructed at a place called Balmoral, a little way along the coast from Mosman, which the Lord was to use as one of his platforms when he came. It was a wonderful site she had chosen. Although only half-finished, the amphitheatre was already being used, and Mother gave one or two public lectures there while she was at the Manor. She was a beautiful speaker. I always enjoyed hearing her speak and was never embarrassed or fearful that she might break down.

Towards the end of May, Bishop Leadbeater consecrated a little temple attached to the amphitheatre, but when the moment came for the lighting of the sacred lamp which was

162

to be the climax of the ceremony, the holy oil was found to be missing. After Bishop's wrath had been passed down through several layers, some old lady's tonic was produced and found to be sufficiently combustible.

CHAPTER TWENTY-FIVE

After Krishna's departure with Nitya to the mountains it became easier for us to concentrate on the business which had brought us to Sydney. Advancements along the spiritual path were said to take place at the great occult festivals. One of the greatest of these was Wesak, which was to fall this year on the night of the full moon of May 8, and to prepare us for taking a step on that night, Bishop, or Brother as we soon learnt to call him, and as I shall call him hereafter (it was only his special young people who were privileged to call him Brother), was giving all his attention to a small group of us, which consisted of Mother, Ruth, Helen, Betty, Monica and me. Mother and Ruth were already Accepted pupils, so the next step for them was the great one of the First Initiation, while Monica and Helen, who were already on Probation, looked forward to being Accepted. For Betty and me it would be the lowly step of Probation, but still it was the first rung of the ladder, and we prepared ourselves for advancement as best we could, chiefly by endeavouring to practise unselfishness. There was much scope for this in our close quarters, but the opportunities were greater for me than for Mother and Betty. They were dreadfully untidy, and as I was very much the reverse, I was kept in a continual state of controlled irritation in our overcrowded room where provisions for tea and supper had to be stored as well as all our belongings.

As an additional help Brother offered to magnetise for us some object which we constantly wore. I gave him my diamond brooch, my only jewel, and he said he would put joyousness into it, the quality I lacked most. In a few days he returned it to me, 'sparkling deliciously' as no jeweller has ever made it sparkle. It really did help me for a time. Whenever I closed my hand over it I felt a rush of joy. This may have been pure imagination, but it was no less effective for that, and its sparkle, which gradually dimmed, was certainly not imaginary.

The special group I have mentioned was summoned every evening into Brother's room, when he would talk or read aloud to us, occasionally breaking into hymns at the top of his tuneless voice. Theodore would also be present, but then he seldom left Brother. He slept in his room and acted as page, valet, messenger boy and ambassador rolled into one. Brother would read mostly ghost stories to us, including *Haunters and the Haunted* by my great-grandfather, Bulwer Lytton, for whom he had a great admiration. (According to him, Bulwer Lytton had been a high Initiate.) He made these stories all the more frightening by his strong belief in ghosts and fairies (or *devas* as he called them, using the Sanskrit word). April 30 was Walpurgis Night and he warned us to be very careful on the astral when we were asleep that night because so many evil spirits would be abroad.

But I found his talk more enthralling than any ghost story. When he felt inclined for conversation the lights would be turned out and the only illumination would come from the gas fire and the transom over the door. He would sit in an upright armchair in his red cassock with its red velvet collar, his elbows on the arms of the chair, the tips of his fingers pressed together and his right knee shaking violently up and down as he talked. In the only comfortable chair in the room, drawn up close beside him, his cat would be sleeping. This cat, a large tortoiseshell, was the one creature at the Manor whom Brother treated with true respect. It was said to be in its last incarnation in the animal kingdom, and already it had a crafty, wicked, human knowingness. One was appalled to think of the kind of man or woman it might turn out to be in its next life.

Brother talked of the sublime and the ridiculous in exactly the same chatty, jovial, loud way. For instance, after telling us that the Virgin Mary, having played her part so wonderfully as the Mother of Jesus (her final incarnation) and being given the choice of where she would like to help in the future, had decided to become a great guardian angel, always close at hand to help women in trouble, sickness and childbirth, so

165

that she was as much the bearer of the sorrows of women as Christ was of the sorrows of men – he would go on in exactly the same tone to tell us how Colonel Olcott (the joint founder with Madame Blavatsky of the Theosophical Society), who had 'preserved to the end the breezier, earlier attitude to the Masters before we knew sufficient to be really reverent,' had one day called the Master Morya 'Daddy'. ('And how did the Master take it?' one of us asked, for naturally we were all eager to know. 'The Master laughed heartily,' Brother replied. 'It quite prostrated me for the moment. We were just in ordinary conversation in the Master's house and the Master was telling him that he should not have done so-and-so, and the Colonel replied, "Well, Daddy, you were responsible for that."') And then again without changing his tone he would go on to tell us how the psychic components of the Sacraments appeared to clairvoyant eyes before and after the Consecration, and then immediately switch to an anecdote, illustrating the need to guard against over-enthusiasm, about a lady of his acquaintance who had tried to help a recently dead friend in his first bewilderment at finding himself in another world. 'I happened to come across them on the astral that night,' he said, 'and there was this lady shooting out great flames of enthusiasm, and her wretched victim flying in front of her quite terrified.' This idea of helping others on the astral plane, especially the newly dead, was not new to me. Mother had told me about it as early as anything I could remember, and had enrolled me in a band of what were called Invisible Helpers.

Brother said during one talk that it would be possible for us young people, if we exerted ourselves to the utmost, to take four Initiations in our present incarnation. If we managed to do that, the strong possibility was that we would become Adepts in our next life, without having to spend the usual seven incarnations in casting off the last five fetters. 'But if you think,' he said, 'that after this life you are going to spend any nice times rolling about in the heaven world in Elysian fields, I am afraid you will be disappointed. In fact you will probably come straight down again into incarnation.'

*   *   *

166

We went for several expeditions with Brother in the first few weeks, to Manly, Bulli Pass and Botany Bay. We never knew beforehand if, or when, we were going, and therefore much of our time was spent hanging about on the verandah outside his room waiting for him to emerge, for to miss the opportunity of an excursion with him was almost a disgrace which might adversely affect one's chances of advancement. Anyone who was on the verandah when he happened to come out of his room in the mood for a walk might be invited to accompany him, so it was most of the Manor community, not only our special group, who spent so much of their time waiting.

One Thursday morning, after going into town for a special church service, I stayed on with Helen to have lunch in a tea-shop called the Golden Gate, where she introduced me to waffles and maple syrup, and then went with her to a cinema. When we got back to the Manor I found that Mother, Ruth and Betty had been out all the afternoon with Brother in his motor-car and that he had asked for me. I felt like breaking down but decided that I would wait to do so until after dinner, and then discovered that I no longer wanted to – a most valuable lesson in self-control.

I found Brother's talk at its most fascinating out of doors. He told us about the life in trees and minerals, and of the nature-spirits and *devas*, invisible to the ordinary eye, who swarmed round us as we walked. As a rule, *devas* resented the presence of human beings, but the ones we came across thought that on the whole we were a better type than the average bank holiday tripper. At least we did not smoke or drink. Tobacco and beer were the two smells that fairies disliked most. There were no deaths, he said, along the *deva* evolution. Fairies gradually drifted into manifestation and their period of life was indefinite. They were sometimes able to change their line of evolution to that of the human, and vice versa, usually through the love of some human being. He told us that rocks and trees were individuals, capable of feeling. A rock in National Park had become very fond of one of the Manor boys and loved him to sit upon it. The life could not leave the rock, but it could all gather at one end as if reaching out its arms, and the life of this particular rock used to reach out towards the boy, seeming to envelop him.

How wonderful, I thought, to inspire love in a tree or a rock – as wonderful as to make the heart of a flower beat faster.

CHAPTER TWENTY-SIX

We soon found out how favoured we were in thus being taken up by Brother. It gave Betty and me great kudos in the Manor community in spite of our low spiritual standing, for the very fact of being taken up so noticeably must mean that we were marked out for speedy advancement. Spiritual snobbery was rife. Money, titles, degrees, ability, counted for nothing, except perhaps with Brother himself, who, being able to create Initiates, had retained a certain respect for lords and ladies, and I cannot help thinking that Mother's title had a little to do with our privileged position. But except by him, the one question asked by everyone was, 'How far advanced are you along the Path?' and there was never any need to answer, for everyone made it his business to find out. Besides, the steps taken were usually made public. They were not put up on a notice board as the results of an examination might be, but the news got round very quickly after one of the great occult festivals.

There was one Dutch boy of nineteen, called Hank, living at the Manor, who had been there for six years without taking a single step, and we were warned by Theodore that we must have no contact with him. He was there with his mother and sister who were well advanced along the Path, but Hank himself had refused to join the Church or Co-Masonry. He was in fact such a hardened individualist that all he cared about was playing the clarinet, for which the Masters had no possible use. (Betty, Helen and Theodore were encouraged to practise the fiddle and the piano, but that was acceptable as it enabled them to play the organ, and violin voluntaries, in church.) Hank must have possessed great strength of charac- ter to withstand the pressure put on him, including the persuasions of his own mother, and the social ostracism must have been hardest of all to resist. He was not exactly sent to Coventry, but we were not allowed to exchange more than the barest civilities with him.

My own week-day occupations, apart from hanging about on the verandah waiting for Brother to emerge, were writing in my diary and teaching myself shorthand and typing. On Sundays we went twice into town for morning and evening services (and sometimes three times when there was a healing service in the afternoon) which as well as the ferry-journey entailed a long tram-ride. Sometimes on a cold wet night the only congregation at St Alban would be the inhabitants of the Manor, and we wondered why we could not have stayed at home and had Vespers and Benediction in our own little chapel, but Brother was insistent on our attendance at Sunday church. He told us that if we could see the wonderful force going up in glowing colours through the church-roof and spreading over the whole city we would realise the importance of this communal worship. We were seriously reprimanded by him when the emanations through the roof were not sufficiently strong or beautifully coloured. Whether he could see them while he was still in the church, or only when he came out, I do not know, but it is a fact that the times when he complained of a lack of force and beauty did happen to coincide with those occasions when I, at any rate, was not giving everything I had to the service.

It is strange that having detested church all through my childhood I should have been happier during the services at St Alban than at any other time while I was in Sydney, especially at Benediction. Certainly a very powerful atmosphere was generated. I loved the smell of incense which came from censers swung by two acolytes, of whom Theodore was invariably one. I was half-hypnotised by the smell and the chanting, and very often lost consciousness — by which I do not mean that I fell asleep, but that I found myself floating away rapturously through the top of my head.

We were encouraged to try and leave our bodies in meditation. We had a session of meditation at least once a day. This did not do me any harm, but it was very harmful to Betty, who anyhow suffered from pains at the top of her head, which became excruciating at times while we were there, and

170

were to trouble her for years afterwards. I do not know how many of the people at the Manor who claimed to be clairvoyant and clairaudient really were so, but there was one small sprite of a boy who, I am convinced, did see things which we could not. It was easy to believe that he was about to change to the *deva* kingdom or had only just become human. At meditation, he told us, he would sometimes project a tube, rather like a canvas fire-escape, down to the sea, and the water-spirits would come running up it and dance about the room. We could see him following their invisible (to us) antics with delighted amusement. If he was deceiving us all he certainly kept up the pretence, week after week, month after month, with a consistency remarkable in a boy of nine.

At Wesak there were seventy advancements in different parts of the world – three more even than Brother had anticipated – forty-five Probations (which made Betty's and my achievement rather unremarkable), two First Initiations, one Second Initiation and the rest Acceptances. Mother and Ruth were the two First Initiates, and Harold the Second. It was a particularly festive day because no one was disappointed and many congratulations were whispered round.

Mother was in a state of elation, as well she might be, for it was a tremendous step she had taken. She had entered 'that wondrous consciousness of the Brotherhood, the governing body of the world, which stretches over the universe from eternity to eternity like a calm and mighty sea,' as Brother described it. We might well wonder, he had said to us, how we were fit to govern the universe, but Initiation was of the ego and we did not know ourselves as egos. Our egos were glorious things, whereas our personalities were merely little toes put down into the world. The ego as a rule was not interested in its lower vehicles, but we must so alter our personalities that our egos did become interested.

Mother had certainly deserved to take this step because she had worked ceaselessly for the movement, writing and lecturing, for fifteen years. Now, however, that she had achieved her main object in coming to Sydney, she felt that she ought to be going home. Ursula was expecting a baby in August, and Father, too, was wanting her back. But it was arranged, with Brother's full approval, that Betty and I should stay on in the hope of taking another step at the Festival of All Saints at the end of October. We were all to join up again at Adyar at the end of November for the Golden Jubilee Convention of the Theosophical Society. Brother would be going there with a large party, and Betty, Ruth, Helen and I could travel with him. He was very insistent that when we finally returned to England in the spring of the following year (1926), Betty and I should be presented at Court and come out with all the conventional trappings, so as to spread the Master's word in Society. It was not suggested, however, that we should cease to be vegetarians or be given the time or opportunity to get to know any of our contemporaries in that world. No doubt he imagined that Mother's name was a passport into Society, whereas in truth she had years ago severed all connection with that world.

Father's consent to our staying on in Sydney without Mother had to be obtained, and came in a very reluctant cable. I have since seen the letter that Mother wrote to him after she received this cable, in which she thanked him for allowing us to stay and assured him that Sydney was very healthy and that the life we were leading had 'everything that makes for interest and amusement'.* I am convinced that Mother wrote this in good faith. She did not see our life at the Manor through my eyes, jaundiced by unrequited love. She saw happy people there; some fun and laughter; friendship and love and human warmth. My first impression that the people there were a drab and mediocre lot had certainly been unjust. Among the young people there was a very high standard of looks. Some of the girls were extraordinarily pretty and the boys nearly all good-looking. As for the standard of intelligence, it was at least average.

Whether I stayed on because I hoped to take another step at All Saints, or because I still hoped to see Nitya again before he left for Ojai, I cannot say at this distance. It was probably for both reasons. All I know for certain is that I did very much want to stay and would have resisted any effort to take me away, unless, of course, Nitya had wanted me to go to Ojai

*She gives this letter in full in her book *Candles in the Sun* (Hart-Davis, 1957).

with him, but that was no longer even a dream. Betty also wanted to stay, for she had formed a very close friendship with Theodore by this time.

Mother was to leave at the beginning of June, and a few days before her departure, Krishna came down from Leura to say goodbye to her. He was dreadfully worried about Nitya and impatient with Mother's exaltation and the absorption of us all in our spiritual progress, even though it was he who had first started us along that road. I think he was really concerned for the first time about Nitya's chances of survival and desperately anxious to get him back to Ojai and another course of Abrams's treatment. The specialist who had gone up to Leura to see him had said he would be fit for the journey by the beginning of July, and therefore cabins were booked for them and Rosalind for July 2. While he was in Sydney, Krishna went to the American Consul to arrange for their re-entry permits, which the Consul assured him would come through in plenty of time.

The 2nd of July. Another month. Would I see Nitya before he left?

Seeing Krishna again re-opened my old wound and disgusted me with my Sydney existence, just as in the old days Nitya had dimmed my imaginary world. Krishna was so much like Nitya in so many ways. They moved in the same climate – that climate which had been enchantment to me ever since I could remember. My hard-won peace turned again to jealous unrest. At the same time I realised how much Krishna himself meant to me, with his beauty and sensitiveness and fierce hatred of mediocrity. He looked so ill and tired. It struck me as strange that he who was to play the lead in this great drama for which we were all rehearsing should seem so aloof from it. He was like a perfect rose – the only really perfect specimen of the season – growing in a beautiful garden, whereas we at best were paper imitations, without scent or colour, manufactured inside stuffy rooms by hands practised to turn out these shoddy counterfeits by the dozen. I suffered a most unpleasant revulsion against myself and my tawdry efforts at self-ennoblement, and longed to return to what I really was. Better surely to be a weed with its own vigorous growth than a sapless simulacrum.

173

But this mood vanished with Krishna's return to the hills, and like a child who has lagged behind and almost got benighted, I turned from rebellious danger and ran to catch up with my Master.

On Whit Sunday, two days before Mother left, she read to us the accounts that Krishna and Nitya had written of Krishna's experience in Ojai in 1922. I learnt from them that after four days of intense agony in his head and neck, during which time he could keep nothing down, Krishna had gone out into the garden in the starlight and sat cross-legged under a pepper tree, and there enlightenment had come to him. Nitya and Rosalind, who were sitting on the verandah watching him, had been conscious of a mighty presence in the garden and had known that the Lord Maitreya was there, and Rosalind had even seen him for an instant – that vision of the divine Bodhisattva for which millions wait through countless incarnations – and her face was transfigured with joy. From that moment there was nothing for them but the service of the Lord. And that rapturous experience had been repeated for Nitya again and again at Ojai, Ehrwald and Pergine. He was constantly replenished by it; his vow of self-dedication constantly renewed. And Rosalind had shared that first great moment with him. Rosalind had looked after Krishna during those four days of physical agony and sickness. She had, as Nitya himself wrote, played the part of a great mother during that time. It was a bond between them that nothing could ever break and in which I could never share. I was humbled and shamed by the puniness of my own love and the insignificance of my idyll on board the *Pilsna*. How petty I must have appeared to Nitya in comparison with Rosalind, transfigured by divine joy. As he wrote, he would never forget that look on her face as she cried out, 'Do you see Him, do you see Him?'

Mother left on June 3. I have a note in my diary: 'Mummie left Tuesday evening!! Feelings too mixed. Betty and I changed the room round and took her bed out and tried to be nice to each other.' We ended by having a really good quarrel which shows that we were closer that evening than we had been for a very long time; but after that one outburst we drifted further apart than ever. Mother before she left had opened a banking account in my name because she feared

174

Betty's generosity, and naturally Betty resented this and hated having to come to me for pocket-money, but it was a good thing for Father, for when the time came for closing the account I found, characteristically, that there was more in it than I had expected.

Nevertheless we did not stint ourselves. I see from my diary that we bought Monica 'a beautiful volume of Shelley' for her birthday, and Theodore 'a glorious and gruesomely illustrated Edgar Allan Poe' for his, which cost two guineas and left us without enough money that month to pay the milkman.

CHAPTER TWENTY-SEVEN

A few days after Mother's departure, Rosalind came down to Sydney to do some shopping and spent the night at the Manor. In the evening she sought me out in our room. It was my first meeting with her. She was tall and on the plump side, with fair, wavy hair, splendid teeth, a lovely complexion and eyes of the most unusual blue, like a Siamese cat's. Moreover she had a very gentle voice and the prettiest American accent I have ever heard. But above all she radiated warmth. I remembered Nitya telling me that when he first saw her something seemed to break inside him. I felt more as if a great hardness had suddenly melted. I had discovered that she was tremendously popular at the Manor, and I understood the reason for it the moment I set eyes on her.

She asked me if I would come and sleep with her in the room she shared with Ruth and Helen at the top of the house. I carted my bedding up there and spent the night on the floor beside her bed. I suppose Helen and Ruth were there but I have no recollection of them. It seems to me that I was alone with her. I did not know how much Nitya had told her about me, though he must have told her something for her thus to seek me out. He might merely have told her that he had made my spiritual welfare his responsibility; he must certainly have told her something about helping me because she said at once how pleased he was when he heard I had been put on Probation and how he hoped I would soon be Accepted. (She herself was already an Accepted pupil.)

She told me that he had been very ill indeed when he first arrived; she had feared he would not pull through, but now he was distinctly better and out of danger. He wanted to see me before he left, and a day would be fixed for me to go up to Leura to see him and spend the night.

176

She made me feel that the only thing that mattered was to get him well, and that as she was more fitted by age, if nothing else, to look after him (she was twenty-three to my sixteen), and as for some reason he always did what she told him, it was more suitable for her to nurse him. She did not exactly put all this into words but it was implicit in what she said.

Gradually she smoothed out my jealousy. It was as if the hard corrugations of my heart were being gently ironed out by a loving warmth. Yet I did not confide in her – principally, I think, because I could not have borne to hurt her, and if Nitya had not told her everything about me I did not want to be the one to do so. It seemed to me extraordinary, now I had met her, that his affection could for one instant have strayed from her to me. No doubt it had seemed extraordinary to him too as soon as he saw her again, or perhaps he had begun to feel it long ago – as long ago as when he first went up to Ootacamund and failed to write to me in Delhi. (I was still sure that he had loved me those last two days at Adyar before we went to Delhi.) She was so immeasurably superior to me in every way that he would have been mad not to love her best. If I had been younger I should almost certainly have fallen in love with her myself. She was soft and loving and lovely, and wonderfully motherly. If only I had met her sooner.

She gave me an understanding of those women in history who were equally beloved by men and women. They too must have possessed this supreme gift of defeating jealousy. Rosalind has ever since been a model to me of what a beautiful woman can be – and how few are! She made me feel genuinely glad that Nitya had the comfort of her presence in his illness.

For a long time after this it was my ambition to nurse a man I loved through a dangerous illness, but when the experience eventually came to me, fifteen years later, as things so often do when we want them enough, and I discovered what a devastatingly unromantic business it is, my last lingering envy of Rosalind left me, for I had remained envious of her even though I had ceased to be jealous. Only then did I realise that those months of nursing Nitya must have contained infinitely more pain than joy, and that the praise of her I had heard on all sides for what she was doing for him was fully justified. Till then I had thought to myself, 'What! Praised for doing something I would give my very eyes to do!'

After Rosalind went back to the hills I lived for a summons to Leura, which I was sure would come. I knew it would be my last meeting with Nitya, perhaps for years, and I was determined so to acquit myself that if ever he thought of me in the future it would not be with shame for having for a moment loved me. I knew that the meeting would be an ordeal and not a pleasure, but I was thankful to have the opportunity of appearing at the end in a dignified light, for I was acutely aware now of how often I must have cut a poor figure in front of him. I also hoped that he might say something to clear up the mystery of his change of heart. He had once told me that I would understand if I was twenty. Was there really some clear understanding which only age could give me? (The simplest explanation that he had never really loved me, that I had merely been the victim of a shipboard romance, was one I could *not* accept.) But the hope of having the mystery explained was only a secondary consideration. Above all I wanted to show him that I was different.

The summons came. They were sailing on a Wednesday and I was to go up on the Monday and stay the night. I still had a fortnight, and I resolved in those intervening days to change myself so radically that I would become in reality the person I intended to appear before him. I strove far harder to do this than I had ever striven to make myself acceptable to the Masters. And, of course, I had already changed to a certain extent from the person I was when Nitya and I had last spoken to each other on that bright afternoon so very long ago when he had kissed me. I looked different for one thing, for although I used no make-up – I do not think any of us did at this date – I had just put up my hair. It was parted in the middle (all good Theosophists had a middle parting, I never discovered why) and scraped back into a bun, not very becoming, I imagine, but at least it was an improvement on my pigtails and made me look years older.

So much for the outward change, but inwardly I was more grown up too. For one thing I had now read the accounts of Krishna's experience at Ojai which had affected me profoundly, and for another I had recently come across some

178

lines of poetry which had helped me to reorientate myself, as poetry can sometimes do so magnificently: 'Before the wheat becomes bread it must be ground; before the grapes become wine they must be crushed.' It was a help to think that the crushing, grinding anguish I had been through was an essential process in the formation of the fine, wise, mature person I intended to become, and hoped I already was in embryo. The one thing I could not summon to my aid was a sense of humour.

Krishna came down two or three times from Leura and stayed at Myola. He was always a disturbing influence and yet it was joy to see him. He was sorry that he had made difficulties for us earlier on, and was now doing his very best to be nice to everybody, but he could not help being himself, and Brother did not welcome him, as was apparent to us all. Here already was an indication that he was not going to fit much longer into the pattern laid down for him, and that the leaders of the Theosophical Society who had originally proclaimed him would be the first to repudiate him.

He looked so tired and worried these days that my heart was wrung for him, and I felt more natural and at my ease with him than I had ever done before. I wrote about him at this time, 'Why is he always so delicious? He makes me feel more unselfish than anyone. I wish I could love everyone as purely as I love him.' One evening after a session with Brother in his room, I came back to our own room to find Krishna lying fast asleep on my bed. I had never seen anything so beautiful as his sleeping face, and I felt that my bed had been blessed. Although I knew how reprehensible it was to miss an opportunity of being with Brother, I was sore at heart to think I might have been with Krishna instead.

And then suddenly their sailing date was put forward. I have forgotten why. Perhaps a cabin suddenly became free, or their entry-permits into America came through sooner than was expected – but, for whatever reason, they were to sail a week earlier, and my visit to Leura was off.

It was a blow that crushed the very last drop of juice out of the grape. I think I minded it more than anything that had yet happened in connection with Nitya, and that is to say in the whole of my life. Now I should never have a chance to erase the poor impression he must have of me.

But I did see him for a moment on the morning of his departure, June 24. I was allowed to go on board and say goodbye to him in his cabin on the *Sierra*. He had grown a full black beard which was a shock to me, but he looked rather fine, like a Rajput. In a turban he would have looked magnificent. It was dark in the cabin and I stood while he sat. We did not so much as shake hands. He said to me, 'You have changed,' and his eyes searched my face with a kind of appeal. I must have appeared to him very much older that day, because as well as my hair being up I was wearing a navy-blue coat, made in Delhi, which he had not seen before, severely cut with a high Russian collar.

I asked him how he was and he told me he was better. He then said, 'Have you forgiven me?' a question which took me utterly by surprise, but I replied as if by reflex, 'There is nothing to forgive.' (How many million times must that bleak little exchange with its false response have put an end to all hope?) What did he think he had done to need my forgiveness? Pretended to love me? Loved me for a moment and then changed? Failed in courage to tell me the truth? Hidden behind his illness to avoid an explanation with me? I longed to ask him what he thought he had done (his question had confused me more than ever), but there was no time. I had been told I must stay only five minutes; and besides I had promised myself not to become personal. But if I had gone up to Leura, should I have discovered the truth? Should I then have been able to resist the temptation of asking for an explanation?

The door opened. Others were waiting to say goodbye to him. I suppose I had been with him about three minutes. I had been allowed to go in first, but I might have had longer if I had gone last. We did not shake hands even in farewell, and yet I knew he was reluctant to see me go (how did I know? I just *knew*) and that meant more to me than any touch. I went down the gangway so blind with tears that I had to hold on to the rail for guidance, but at least there was the satisfaction of knowing that I had held them back while I was with him. Thank God I had acquitted myself with dignity. I had recovered my self-respect. But how infinitely more I loved him. I had entered a new dimension of love.

180

I stood with the others on the quay waiting for the ship to pull out, and to my joy and surprise Nitya came up on deck. He had his overcoat collar turned up round his ears. I do not know who, if anyone, stood beside him, for I saw no one but him. (I did not see Rosalind on board at all, though she must have been there.) Streamers were distributed among the passengers and Nitya threw his to me. I caught it, and as the ship drew slowly away from the side we did not take our eyes off each other.

Our purple paper ribbon was drawn taut; it snapped. I was released. It was the end.

CHAPTER TWENTY-EIGHT

Betty and I stayed on at the Manor until the middle of November. Our routine continued unchanged – Mass before breakfast, Vespers and Benediction in the evening; twice into Sydney on Sundays for church. There was, however, less hanging about on the verandah waiting for Brother to come out. During the winter months of July and August, walks and expeditions stopped, and if we saw Brother at all we were sent for to his room after tea, so that the day was our own and we could go out without fear of missing an opportunity of being with him.

Very occasionally we went into Sydney for a cinema; we saw one play – Galsworthy's *The Skin Game* – and went to one Kreisler concert, and a couple of times to the roller-skating rink.

During the long, long Australian winter (or did it just seem long?) boredom engulfed me for the first, and, I am thankful to say, the only time in my life. Boredom is not a question of having nothing to do, but of not wanting to do anything. It is in many ways worse than unhappiness. I was empty. I had felt too much in the last year, and what a year it had been!

I had not lost my belief in the Masters, but I was so apathetic that if I had been told that Jesus Himself was to speak at Dr Rocke's amphitheatre I doubt whether I should have felt more than a flicker of interest.

My chief exertion was going for walks by myself over the rocks between Mosman and Balmoral, but my imagination no longer roamed free as in the old days. (Yet what a setting this might have been for Dicon! He would certainly have added smuggling to his other activities.) I concentrated on jumping from rock to rock and became rather expert at it, and after a few weeks hardly ever fell and skinned my knees on the barnacles. To hurt oneself was a crime in Brother's eyes. One's body was an animal entrusted to one's care and to harm it in any way was as bad as allowing a horse to get a saddle-sore. I have never quite got away from this feeling of being disgraced if I happen to hurt myself. I still expect reproof rather than sympathy.

Out on the rocks I frequently looked at my watch. I lived for meals and consequently grew fat. I always seemed to be hungry and would consume a whole bag of peanuts every time we crossed to Sydney in the ferry. The Mackays, who lived at Myola where Krishna and Nitya had stayed, were wonderfully kind to me and asked me to go up to meals with them whenever I liked. Mrs Mackay was a superb cook and I look back on the meals I had in her house as the best I have ever eaten. Certainly I have never enjoyed food as much as I did at Myola. Mrs Mackay kept a dozen or more large square tins of biscuits in her pantry, and between meals I would often slip in there and gorge myself on ginger-nuts, Bourbons and cream fingers. Gluttony and boredom are amicable twins. If boredom were a state within one's control, I should say it was one of the worst sins on earth, but I believe it to be a disease – a disease of the spirit – no more culpable than anaemia, and far more difficult to cure or alleviate.

Except for one Tasmanian girl, I hardly spoke to anyone, and made no real friends, although there were so many to choose from; but I did become very fond of Helen that winter and more and more appreciative of her good qualities. We were never intimate though. I had no heart left to give to anybody and found that life without love was like food without salt, a hackneyed simile but I can think of no other that so well expresses my sense of flatness and lack of interest in the daily dishes of experience set before me.

Hank, the Dutch boy who played the clarinet, was the only person at the Manor who very slightly attracted me, but he was beyond the pale. One Sunday, coming back from church, he asked me to get off the ferry with him at the Zoo, the stop before Mosman, and walk back to the Manor through the bush. Against my conscience I said yes and hoped we would be able to get off unnoticed, but to my consternation I found that Brother and Theodore were also getting off at the Zoo

183

that day. It occurred to me to stay on the boat after all, but Brother had already seen me moving towards the side and I was sure he had read my intentions; and besides it would have been too cowardly. I felt he would judge cowardice even more severely than disobedience.

Hank and I allowed Brother and Theodore to go on ahead of us, and then walked slowly after them along the bush path. Hank told me of his ambition to become a musician and of his unhappiness at the Manor. I asked him why he could not conform, and he replied that he did not, and could not, believe in the Masters or in any of the other things Brother taught us, and yet he could not get away because he had no money and nowhere to go and his mother refused to leave. I felt very sorry for him but despised him a little at the same time. Surely being a boy it would have been comparatively easy for him to run away, especially from a great port like Sydney?

The next morning I had no smile from Brother at breakfast. He looked right through me and I knew I was in deep disgrace. I wondered how this was going to affect my chances of taking the next step and very much regretted my walk with Hank. No word was said to me about it but I was out of favour with Brother for a week.

For the most part Brother was genial enough but he could be both rude and severe. Several times I heard him roaring at people if he was kept waiting for a few moments. He was a most impatient man and became particularly restive when he was not monopolising the conversation. He could swear lustily on occasion, and was very rude once to a nice young lady who came to take a photograph of him in the garden of the Manor surrounded by such of his young people who had taken some step or other along the Path. She asked him politely if he would mind withdrawing his attention from his cat, who was prowling around and whose movements he was following with his eyes, to which he retorted in a loud voice, 'The cat is so much more interesting than the photographer.'

And on another occasion when we were with him in his car, being seen off from the front door by some of the Manor community, he shouted at them in an angry voice, 'What are you gaping idiots staring at?' But apart from an occasional

184

black look when we were late for breakfast or made a noise in the dining-room, and that one week when I was in disgrace, he was never anything but courteous to Betty and me.

I wish I could discover the truth about him. I doubt whether it will ever be known now. I believed in him implicitly while we were at the Manor, and even today I find it impossible to disbelieve in him altogether. It is much too easy to write him off as a charlatan. It would be the judgment of a fool. I am convinced that he was at least a genuine clairvoyant, though he may not have seen quite all he told us about – but in that case he had the most remarkable imagination. He was undoubtedly a great man. One could not think of him in a subordinate position or in one without power. He had infinitely more power in a Church he had more or less created, and certainly controlled, than if he had attained to a bishopric in the Church of England. The thing that surprises me most about him is that he had achieved so little before, at the mature age of thirty-seven, he met Madame Blavatsky, but perhaps he was a late developer, or maybe he needed the particular channel of Theosophy as an outlet for his great capacities. Or perhaps Madame Blavatsky really did change his whole character in seven weeks, as he claimed. My own guess is that it was the development of genuine clairvoyance which gave him his strange power.

His radiation of mental and physical health was really extraordinary. The very pores of his skin seemed to sparkle with well-being, as if his whole body loved him. Whatever else he was or was not he was a supremely happy man.

I should have said that he was without carnal vices – at any rate by the time I knew him. I saw no sign of immorality of any kind while we were at the Manor. There were plenty of romantic attachments but sensuality was taboo. Our lower selves were certainly starved, and if they dropped out and took up their abode anywhere it was probably in Brother's cat.

Brother had won the love as well as the reverence and respect of his little community; the Manor seemed completely dead on the one occasion when he went away for a few days, and we rejoiced to have him back; but whether his teaching did more harm than good must depend on the individual pupil. I can speak only for myself when I say that I would not have exchanged those months with Brother, unhappy though they were, for any other training in the world – and yet I think my idea of hell would be to find myself back there again.

I struggled along with my shorthand and typing that winter, and kept up my diary, but these occupations were no more than time-killers. My most difficult task was in writing home every week, especially to Nanny and Granny. There was absolutely nothing to say, and yet I felt I owed it to Brother to make out that I was happy and fully occupied. The only real enjoyment (apart from eating) I can remember between Nitya's departure and the end of October was reading *Marius the Epicurean*. As soon as I had finished it I read it again with increased delight. Its charm now eludes me but I have retained a sentimental fondness for the slim red book I bought in Sydney which bears the inscription on the flyleaf: 'Mary. A present from herself on her 17th birthday, July 31, 1925.' I have no recollection of receiving any other presents on that day.

Occasionally and quite unexpectedly a flash of hope would streak through my despondency and I would know for the instant it lasted that somewhere in the future happiness awaited me; and then the brown porridgy mists would close in again and there would still be another hour and a half to get through before lunch. Some years later Father was given by an architectural association a leather-bound *Encyclopaedia Britannica*. It was the first time I had seen these volumes and I was immediately struck by the title of one of them – *Maryb to Mushe*. I knew at once what Mushe was – my winter in Sydney. I made up my mind then that one day I would write an account of my childhood and first love and call it just that, *Maryb to Mushe*.*Maryb (I pronounced it Mary-b) was my fairy self jumping about the nursery in the firelight pretending to fly: Mushe was apathy, dullness of brain and spirit, the skins of the grape after crushing, the husks of the wheat after grinding.

*My publisher would not allow me to use this title.

I stirred a little when spring came, and returned to my more or less normal sentient self when it became really hot. One day I saw a canary sitting on a telegraph wire against a brilliant blue sky as a sparrow might have sat in England – except that the sky in England could never be quite so blue – and I wanted to cry with the sudden rush of happiness that tingled through me. I have never forgotten that tender little yellow bird, that symbol of joy. It was the nicest thing I saw in Australia.

Some savour was returned to life that spring by a serious young man from Lancashire, called Ralph, newly arrived from England as attendant-companion to a rich English cripple in search of spiritual advancement. Ralph had a charming soft accent and a lovely singing voice. He used to sing romantic Victorian songs to me on the ferry going to and from church. He might have gone a long way as a crooner, and now I come to think of it he did look very much like a young Bing Crosby and had some of the same quality in his voice. Neither he nor his crippled friend was allowed to stay at the Manor (Brother ignored them almost completely) and therefore I was able to pass on to Ralph crumbs from the high table. I had the illusion that I was helping him along the Path, that at last I had a disciple of my own, but in truth he was far more dedicated and spiritually minded than I was.

CHAPTER TWENTY-NINE

On the night of the full moon of October 31, the Festival of All Saints, Betty and I were Accepted by our Master. We had been told that we were likely to take this step and must try to get to sleep early because, although the Festival itself was not until 3 a.m., we must be at the Master's house in plenty of time. The result was that I do not think we slept at all. It was so hot now that for the last week or so we had been sleeping out on the verandah, but on this important night we thought we would sleep better indoors. It was so stifling in our room, though, that at about midnight we dragged our mattresses back on to the verandah. But there sleep would not come any more than indoors. The crickets in the garden kept up a terrific clatter; the ferries hooted; other bodies lying out on the verandah snored abominably; and at two o'clock the Greek fishermen round the bay began to sing *I Found a Rose in the Devil's Garden*. Betty got up soon after this and had a bath and then lay down again with cold wet towels wrapped round her legs in an attempt to get the blood down from her head.

But I suppose we must have slept in the end, because Theodore came in in his dressing-gown early next morning to tell us that all had gone well. He himself had taken his Second Initiation. He also told us what other advancements had occurred, so I had the pleasure of giving Ralph the news that he had been put on Probation before he was officially told.

We were very gratified by our success, though not so much I think, as we would have been chagrined had we failed. (If I had failed and not Betty, I should have known that it was due to my disobedience over Hank.) Now that we were Accepted pupils we could join the E.S. (the Esoteric Section of the Theosophical Society), and a few days later we went to our first E.S. meeting in the Theosophical lecture-hall in town.

The pictures of the Masters (copies of Mrs St John's portraits), which were usually hidden behind a golden curtain, were uncovered and the floor was strewn with rose-petals and lilies of the valley. We had to recite the E.S. pledges in turn (I have no recollection of what they were) and were each given an armful of secret pamphlets to take away with us.

Before we left Sydney, a small party of us, at Betty's suggestion, went up to Dr Rocke's house at Leura in the Blue Mountains for a week-end. This was the house where Nitya had stayed. It was called Nilgiri, and I was surprised to find that it was hardly more than a log cabin. We had intended that our party should consist of no one who was less than an Accepted pupil (Betty and I were now as snobbish as the rest), but as Brother would not let us go without a chaperone, and as one of the required status was not available, we were obliged to take someone who was not even on Probation. This was Mrs Merton, formerly one of Father's rich clients. It was she who had lent us Folly Farm in that golden summer of 1916. Mother had converted her to Theosophy, and here she was, haggard, dowdy, with cropped hair and none of the accoutrements of her former style of living, although she had not lost any of her money. She had appeared in Sydney after Mother left, wanting to be 'brought on' by Brother, but there was no room for her at the Manor and she was living in lodgings somewhere in Mosman, hoping to catch an occasional glimpse of the great man. Even at that time hers struck me as a tragic case and I could not help feeling how greatly the spiritual life had diminished her. How infinitely more admirable had been Father's 'Mertoni' with her appreciation of good food and lovely surroundings. Plump and soignée, her white hair beautifully dressed by her French maid, her frills and furbelows crisply starched, she had been a woman to command respect anywhere. It hurt me to see her as she was now, for she had been wonderfully kind to us as children. It was she who had taken us to *Peter Pan* every year and invited us to many Christmas parties. Mother had also converted Miss Dodge, but the latter had wisely remained in her own luxurious setting and yet had not been forgotten when the spiritual rewards were doled out at the occult festivals. The fact that neither Mrs Merton nor the rich

cripple was ever taken up by Brother, although they would
have given anything for a little attention from him, seems to
prove that he was not influenced in his choice of disciples by
their money, as some of his detractors have tried to make out.

It rained the whole time we were at Leura, but I was happy
on the tiny verandah I had to myself, reading my E.S. papers
and savouring my new relationship with my Master, who, by
accepting me, had opened his consciousness to mine so that I
could now draw at will upon his strength.

I thought very little about Nitya, although I might have
been sleeping in the very verandah, in the very bed, he had
used, but when we got back to the Manor I was overjoyed to
find a cable congratulating us on the step we had taken,
signed, 'With love. Krishna. Nitya.' Brother must have cabled
them the results of All Saints.

It was the first word I had heard from either of them since
they left, but I had not been waiting for a letter or hoping for
one. I did not expect to hear. I hoped now, however, that
Nitya was really pleased with me, and I wondered whether I
could still make him the happiest man in the world by taking
my First Initiation. It would be something to live for if I could
believe it was true.

We had a household meeting on the eve of our departure
for India. These meetings took place nearly every week and
usually ended by a resolution being passed to practise strict
economies all round, but on this occasion Brother congratu-
lated those few who were staying behind to carry on the work
of running the Manor and assured them that they were
building up very good *karma* for themselves by doing so.
There was a hint here that they would not be forgotten at the
next festival.

We sailed for Colombo on the *Oronsay* on November 14, a
huge party of us in the care of Brother who gallantly
acknowledged the responsibility of travelling with 'such a
bevy of beauty'. Mother was to meet us at Colombo. She had
left England ten days before. Travelling with her were Mrs
Besant, who had been in London giving another series of
lectures at Queen's Hall, Krishna and Rosalind. It was
thought that Nitya was well enough to be left, and in their
absence Madame de Manziarly had gone to Ojai to take care

of him. (I had learnt this from Mother's letters.) It was very important that Krishna should attend the Jubilee Convention at Adyar, since it was generally understood that the Lord was to speak through him for the first time in public at one or other of the Convention meetings, and no doubt it was felt also that Rosalind must not be allowed to miss this stupendous event.

We got to Melbourne late the following evening and stopped there the whole of the next day. In the morning we all went ashore to have a look at the town and then lunched in a tea-shop and went to a cinema. In the late afternoon there was to be an E.S. meeting at the local Theosophical hall at which Brother was to preside.

Just before the meeting Theodore came and told me jauntily that Nitya was dead.

At the meeting Brother announced that he had just received a telegram from Mrs Besant from Port Said breaking the news of Nitya's death. There was nothing to be sad about, he said. It was all for the best, for it was forwarding the work of the Masters, and Nitya would speedily take a new and more suitable body because he was much needed. 'It is only human that we should be unhappy at the death of someone we love very much,' he said, 'but we are trying to be *superhuman*.'

I did not feel at all superhuman, and after the meeting I got hold of Dr Rocke, who seemed to be the most sympathetic person available, and asked her whether in his new body Nitya would remember the past. She replied briskly, 'What does that matter? He doesn't need to remember the past. All is future now.'

When I got back to the ship I found a cable addressed to me, also from Port Said, saying, 'Nitya peacefully passed away. Love. Mother. Krishna.'*

I got quickly into my bunk (I had the luxury of a small cabin to myself on this journey) and pulled the bedclothes up over my head.

So Nitya was dead. I could not have shed a tear. I was dry, dry, dry. I told myself that I was glad his sufferings were over.

It began to get rough almost as soon as we started. The cabin

*The fact that this cable was addressed to me and not to Betty or to both of us makes me think that Mother must have known about my feelings for Nitya, unless it was Krishna who suggested sending it. He certainly knew.

191

creaked and groaned and I knew I should soon begin to feel sick. But greatly to my surprise I did not feel so much as a moment's queasiness, although it got very rough indeed during the night.

So Nitya was dead. Our philosophy did not hold with the survival of personality. It was his ego only that would be reincarnated. He would remember nothing. It was all over. He was gone and it was all over. He was gone for ever.

Had he ever really loved me? I should never know now.